A WALK ON THE SIDEWALK

By

David William McCormick

This book is a work of non-fiction. Places, events, and situations in this story are true. Some names have been changed to protect their privacy.

ISBN: 1-4033-6552-0 (e-book)
ISBN: 1-4033-6553-9 (Paperback)
ISBN: 1-4033-6554-7 (Dust Jacket)

Library of Congress Control Number: 2002094008

This book is printed on acid free paper.

Printed in the United States of America
Bloomington, IN

1st Books - rev. 04/11/03

True stories and incidents of the Vietnam War as told
by the Command Radiotelephone Operator

November 19, 1968 - November 18, 1969

25th Division, 1st Battalion, 27th Infantry, Bravo Company

By David William McCormick

DEDICATION

This book was written for Dennis. A good person. A very special friend. And my brother. He is someone who believed in me. His support and guidance, patience and understanding provided me with the encouragement to write this. I love you for that.

In remembrance of my friend, my hero, my soul mate. His acrid sense of humor and steady stream of witty letters kept me going and gave me the faith to maintain a belief that there was life after war.

James Charles Morrone

Special Thanks

To Andy Vaught, my former teacher and mentor. Someone whose enthusiasm of reading stimulated me to discover the joys of writing. To my friend Mariano who kept me motivated by continually reminding me that there is a whole young generation who still very much maintain an interest in this tragic conflict. To my second soul mate and special friend. My perpetual cheerleader, my guide, my guru in life, Mr. David Weber of New York City. Also thanks to Erica Noonan and to Cyetta of Wellesley. The assistance and readings and edits and suggestions you both made were truly appreciated. You are a special kind of people. To the Daly's of Wyckoff. Mike, Nina and little Mike. Without a doubt you are my second family. And to Kevin Glavin, a friend I can count on. A friend who is always there for me. A friend… who is always there for me. Lastly, to all the fine members of Bravo Company: to name you all and to thank you all for allowing me the interviews would be a book in itself. But you know who you are and how you contributed, and I thank you for that.

This book is dedicated in the memory of a pleasantly gentle soul whose heart, mind and spirit consisted of all that is good.

Miles Dawson Touchberry, Jr.
of Sumter, SC

Killed in action in the Province of Binh Duong

April 12, 1969

Panel 27W, Row 68 on the Vietnam Veterans Memorial

There were only two requirements necessary in order to carry the captain's radio:

One: "Issue his orders in a clear, precise and understandable way."

Two: "Make damn sure that they are carried out."

Good clear communication was pivotal to the success of any mission. Anything less was a contributor to failure and could be disastrous. A good RTO instinctively knew when, where and what orders were about to be given. In the peak of battle, a good RTO could call in an air strike, a gunship or a round of artillery without blowing his people away along with the enemy. When under fire, a good RTO will not only know who was hit, but how badly. He will do his best to communicate the wounds in detail as he calls in for a 'dust-off' (medevac). He will locate a secure and safe landing zone. He will prioritize who gets evacuated. He will point out who stays behind. As the medevacs lift off, he will see to it that cover and return fire on the enemy is provided. If necessary he will guide the deadly Cobra gun-ships and verbally coordinate and pinpoint the safe zones and the hot zones. Being calm in the face of imminent danger, with people screaming, bullets flying and mortar rounds landing was not a duty or obligation. It was a necessity. Lives depended upon this. I considered myself a good RTO.

It was that August day in 1957 I thought of the most and I supposed kept me going. I was on the Cape at the beach in Truro. With me were my younger sisters, Ann and Laurie. I remember the tide had been out for a while and was at that threatening stage of returning when I felt all would be lost.

We rushed to put the finishing touches on our very own sandcastle that we perceived to be indestructible.

Ann hurriedly pushed more sand around the perimeter, fortifying the walls, in hopes of forestalling the inevitable. Laurie, her young imagination having no bounds, ignored the dangers of the incoming tide as she ever so delicately poured sand into the wax Dixie cup, which, only moments earlier, was filled with lemonade. Gently, she patted the tops of the guard towers that seemed to be so essential in warding off whatever evils that lay beyond the ocean waves.

As for myself, I was positioned directly in front of the castle, which allowed me to focus on the incoming tide. With the waves rushing in, I excitedly called out the necessary warnings, creating a sense of urgency to finish. "Higher on the right," I shouted. "Make the sidewall thicker. We can't last much longer."

I remembered the background sounds of children shrieking as the cool waters rushed in and brushed against their naked feet. The cries from the multitude of seagulls that sailed overhead. The ever present smell of salt in the air. The strength of the late afternoon sun and the warmth of the pleasingly gentle winds that blew across my body.

This is what I thought of. This is what I remembered most.

DAY ONE: GETTING THERE

November 1968

Dearest David,

Thanksgiving will not be the same without you. You have what it takes to survive this and our prayers will be with you. I went out shopping for...

Love,

The Mother

PS - Walk on the sidewalk

I sat in the window seat on the right hand side. It was one of the largest planes I had ever been on. The flight was filled to capacity. With the TWA logo on the tail section, it could have been any other commercial flight flying towards a popular tropical area or vacation spot. The difference was it was a military charter. And with the exception of the stewardesses and the flight crew, all on board were wearing dark green jungle fatigues. The passengers were male and in their teens or early twenties. But we were not heading for a vacation spot. We were en route to a war zone.

The trip lasted about eighteen hours. The civilian flight crew seemed exceptionally attentive. Having made these trips many times before, they did what they could to make us as comfortable as possible, from decks of cards to copies of magazines such as *Life* and *Popular Mechanics*, from pats on the shoulder to small conversation. A stewardess who told us she was from Green Bay, Wisconsin mentioned that her younger brother was just drafted and she hopes he will be okay. Although a number of meals were served during the trip, I didn't have much of an appetite. Time seemed to move quickly and conversation began to circulate among some of the crew members that we would soon be entering the airspace that encompassed the

1

area of South Vietnam. Outside my window, darkness was giving way to sunrise. From this distance, the panoramic view of the jungle slowly came into focus. I experienced a multitude of emotions from excitement and curiosity to tension and fear. Did that small village below belong to the enemy? From the air, the spectacle of the land below was a far cry from my old neighborhood in Westchester County, New York.

The first clue we were arriving in an unfriendly environment was the landing itself in Bien Hoa. We seemed exceptionally high and not at all lined up for a landing. Surely, there must be another landing area I could not see from my vantage point. Then the captain made the following announcement: "Good morning everyone, we hope you had a restful trip. I have just been notified by ground operations that the welcoming committee this morning is not a particularly friendly one."

I heard a few halfhearted chuckles from the forward cabin and some strained laughter when a soldier shouted out that he may be shot at and killed on the very first day. I remember thinking how I despised inside jokes, especially if it pertains to someone shooting at you. The captain continued, "We had some earlier reports of scattered sniper fire, along with a few RPGs." (I would learn later that RPG stood for Rocket Propelled Grenade, the weapon of choice used by the enemy. The target of choice, anything that flies.)

The dramatic reduction in the speed of the plane was at odds with the increased thumping of my heart. And the only thing dropping faster than our altitude was my morale. How the hell did I wind up here? I had a choice. Did I make the wrong one? I had the chance. Why didn't I run? Why didn't I hide? After all, compared to war, how bad could Canada have been? The captain continued, "So at this time, I'm gonna ask the flight crew to take their seats so we can get you on the ground and out of here as fast and quickly as possible." His comments left little to the imagination: our plane had the potential of being a target.

The next few moments were nothing less than terrifying. The captain was making a sharp right turn in order to line up the aircraft with the field. The descent was fast and steep. When we touched down, the flight crew scrambled towards the forward doors. Two attendants per door unfastened the latches and partially opened them as we sped down the runway. It was at this moment the full reality of what was to lie ahead finally hit me. For sure, we were not arriving in a place I wanted to be.

We were ushered off in quick formation. The heat and humidity was our first formal greeting. A somewhat impassive Air Force sergeant was our second. Rushed along, we were led into a large hanger type area that was heavily fortified with sandbags on all sides, with a roof of reinforced steel. The sergeant stood in front on top of a large staging area and did his best to welcome us into the country that would be our new home for the next 365 days. He informed us that over the past 24 hours, the air base had been receiving incoming mortar rounds along with sporadic sniper fire.

Speaking in steady monotones, he clearly cautioned us as to some of the many hazards that were to lie ahead. "When in the swamps, don't be surprised when your body is covered with blood-sucking leeches. When in an open field that might remind you of a place back home, be aware that you may find yourself to be the target of an enemy sniper or even the focal point of a series of incoming mortar rounds." He also said he believed we were well trained by the United States military and that we should be able to handle whatever situation might arise. Our group of 350 plus, from differing backgrounds, walks of life and education, listened intently as the sergeant gave his oration about health and safety and the extreme conditions we were about to face. For a brief period of time he spoke about wounds he himself had suffered and even briefer on the subject of the recent death of a friend. Without exception, we listened to every word. His comments led us all to the realization of one simple fact: from here on in, our lives were truly at risk.

The sergeant held a clipboard and some large folders in his left hand. A .45 caliber automatic hung on the right side of his belt. (His face told a story in itself; eyes darting from left to right, a number of wrinkles you would not expect to see on someone of his age gave him the impression of being overwrought.) I wondered why he appeared to be so haggard at this time of day and wondered if it was something more menacing. He also said if anyone were to call out the word "incoming" we should immediately run for the underground bunker that lay directly behind him, adding, if we did get hit with incoming mortar fire, the only thing we would see prior to the explosion would be his "fucking ass," as he'd be the first to dive into the bunker. (So much for pleasantries I thought).

"Another word, gentlemen. If we take a hit, I am not going to hold your hand and lead you to safety. YOU ARE OFFICIALLY IN A COMBAT ZONE," he shouted. "Some of the big wigs back in Washington call this a conflict. Some are calling it a skirmish. Call it what you will. But make no mistake, this… is… a war!

"People, listen up," he continued. "This is very important. The South Vietnamese are our friends. They are our allies. They are not the enemy. The North Vietnamese has their own army. They are called NVA. They are disciplined, organized and highly regimented. Gentlemen, 'they' are the enemy" (as a new recruit, I was glad I was told who the enemy was.) "You have been sent here by the United States Government to fight for and defend this country. You were sent here to stop the North Vietnamese from infiltrating and taking over this country. You were sent here to defend and fight for democracy."

He continued. "Besides the NVA, you will be fighting another enemy. They are called Viet Cong. Gooks. Guerrillas." (Although listening intently, I wondered if these were all one and the same or three different groups, making it a total of four separate enemies we would be up against. I became a tad apprehensive.) "We call these people 'Charlie' for short. These people are South Vietnamese. They have turned on their country and are fighting locally for the north. They are what we call enemy sympathizers." (Oh, that's just wonderful, I thought, an 'in-house' enemy!)

"They look, talk, act, walk, sit, run, smile, eat and shit just like the locals," he added. (I wondered how he knew the latter.) "Do not mistake them for friendlies," he yelled out. "There are only two things that separate the local villagers from Charlie. Number 1, Charlie sleeps during daylight hours, and number 2, Charlie likes to kill, injure, maim, harass, and cause bodily harm to you GIs. If you are in the unenviable position of being in the wrong place at the wrong time, you may trip on one of the many VC mines or booby traps that Charlie has set. You may be shot. Or worse, a barrage of enemy mortar fire may hit you. Should this be the case, do not panic. And if you see that your blood is red do not be alarmed. That is normal. Are there any questions?"

Silence from the group.

BEYOND THE WIRE

November 1968

Dearest David,

Life in Westchester just became a little more exciting. Your father came home last night. Told him I wanted the house painted. He said yes. Asked him for a new car. He said yes. Then asked him for a new coat. He said yes to that also. Since he was in a yes mood, asked him for a divorce. Attorneys getting together next week...

Love,

The Mother

PS - Walk on the sidewalk

I was assigned to the 25th Division, 1st Battalion, 27th Infantry and on Friday November 22, I arrived by convoy at the base camp known as "Mahone." It was located approximately 30 miles north of Saigon and just on the outskirts of the town of Dau Tieng. The campgrounds were round and roughly the size of a football field. The outer edges, lined with endless layers of barbed wire, gave it a foreboding appearance. Positioned ninety feet apart were three-foot-high stacks of green burlap sandbags, which made up the numerous underground bunkers. Located in the center of the camp was a much larger bunker that stood about ten feet high. To its right was a large tent. Its side flaps were open displaying several small groups of men who were eating. A short distance from the tent I observed two men standing on a raised wooden platform. They were nude and lathered up with soap. They rotated in turn in order to catch the single stream of water that trickled down from the large olive green burlap water bag that was suspended overhead. To the far left was sort of a mini-camp within. A small wall of sandbags separated it from the rest of

5

the camp. In the center were a half dozen or so large 105 mm artillery guns pointed in different directions.

The camp itself was completely devoid of vegetation. Just dirt and sand intermingled with rolls upon rolls of barbed wire which encompassed the perimeter. As I jumped down from the truck carrying a dozen other guys into camp, a sergeant began calling out names. His name was Ron Risley, and being older at the age of 26, went by the nickname of "Gramps." He had a pleasant smile and seemed well organized. (Within three months' time and just after an intense firefight inside the Michelin Rubber Plantation, Sergeant Ronald R. Risley would be offered, but would not accept, the honor and privilege of a battlefield commission.) He began to call out names. "Flanders, C Company," "Kowolski, C Company," "Hendricks, artillery," "McCormick, B Company." After completing the roll call, the sergeant walked us around the camp familiarizing us with the different companies and facilities. He pointed out the latrines, the medical tent, munitions bunker and the mess tent. The big bunker in the middle was the headquarters command center. As we came across the mini-camp that contained the large artillery guns, he cautioned us and said that no matter what the situation, you never want to walk in front of them. He told us you never know when they are going to fire and you never know when a round may misfire or fall short. He mentioned the entrance and exit to the Mahone base camp were one and the same and it would be suicide to make an attempt to cross the wire at any other point. The reason for this was some of the surrounding perimeter was fortified and protected by explosive mines.

Halfway through the tour of the base camp the sergeant came across two men, one of whom was laying telephone ground wire. Briefly pausing, he called out, "This is B Company," and left me as he continued on the tour with the others. After a few moments, the one laying the wire slowly approached me and said, "You must be the FNG. That's military talk for Fuck'n New Guy and you're gonna hear it a lot so you better get used to it." He was about my height, had dark dirty blond hair, brown eyes and fair skin, a handsome guy who displayed a sort of cynical smile as he extended his hand. "John Paxson," he said. "I'm the captain's RTO" (radiotelephone operator).

"We heard we were getting some replacements. Guess you're one of them," John said, then added, "Oh, and I guess you should get to know this guy," referring to the fellow next to him. He's the M-60 operator for the 3rd platoon. If you are at all like me when you arrived in country, you'll need interpretation. That's a machine gun operator. "Pow, Pow, Pow, Pow," John said in a kidding manner while pointing his two index fingers and pretending they were machine guns. "A dirty job but a good person to have around if things get messy. His name is Pete Arnone. Pete, meet…you do have a name, I take it?"

John was the very first person I met while out in the field who was, to an extent, civilized to me. I felt I must have come across as a character out of Mayberry RFD. For being in a war zone, I was in awe of John's good manners and calm demeanor. I introduced myself to John and Pete. Pete was a big guy and reminded me of one of the captains of The Halstead School's football team where I had attended high school. At first, Pete intimidated me. But when he told me he was from New York, I knew at some point there would be a bond between us. John took the time to show me around. He introduced me to the company medic, named Miles Touchberry, along with the 3rd platoon RTO named Roger Wasson. He took me over to the supply bunker where I registered the serial number of my M-16. I was introduced to a very large shirtless black man named Green. Green cautioned me that since we were at war, if I ever lost or misplaced my weapon I would be given a court-martial and a dishonorable discharge. John, who I later learned did not like to use foul language, leaned over and whispered in my ear, "Horse droppings. If that were the case I would have been out of here months ago." I was also given a new set of fatigues, a pair of shorts, jungle T-shirts and socks along with a knapsack and insect repellent. My company would supply ammunition.

After I gathered all my supplies I felt comfortable enough to ask John what I should expect to happen over the first few days. He told me not to worry too much since I was too new to go out on ambush and that I needed to get acclimated to the new surroundings. He added in all probability, I would be digging bunkers and filling sandbags until they felt I was ready to take part in a mission. John introduced me to a few others including the first sergeant where I learned the majority of the company was on an overnight ambush mission with three of the platoons. The first sergeant, commonly referred to as "Top," added that if there were no encounters with the enemy in the next 24 hours the company would be returning sometime tomorrow afternoon.

As the day wore on I met a few more people from my 3rd platoon. With evening upon us I was informed I could sleep in a bunker if I wished, but most slept outside on top or along side of them as they were poorly ventilated and uncomfortably hot inside. Still not sure of my ground and for safety sake, I chose the bunker and stayed inside until 1 AM when the heat got to me. Grabbing my poncho liner, I moved outside and stretched out on top of the bunker. There, under the stars, a cool evening breeze lulled me to sleep. The night was quiet. The morning of my second day, with no particular assignment given me, I roamed the inside of the base camp. The looks and stares I received from a good number of the men I passed were puzzling at first until I heard from a distance one of them call out "FNG."

Passing by the medical tent I saw a number of the local women, who I would learn to refer to as Mama-sans, sitting on some crudely improvised benches. I was surprised to see the children around them were being examined and treated by the military medical personnel. A baby was getting a shot, a little girl was having her throat examined, a boy, no older than four or five, was touching a bandage that was freshly wrapped around his thigh. He was wiping away tears as the one who had done the bandaging pulled a batch of lollypops from his jacket and pretended to eat them before passing them on to his young charge.

Wandering away from the various goings-on and not being 100 percent attentive to where I was going, I found myself standing alongside a roll of barbed wire that had separated us from the outer limits of our campsite. Looking out beyond the wire, first north, then east, then south, all I could see was a wide, open clearing that extended half a mile or more up to the surrounding wood lines. It would be difficult indeed for someone to sneak up at night without being detected. There was absolutely no cover whatsoever outside the wire.

Looking west and by the main entrance was an entirely different setting. It had very little clearing and was only a few hundred feet from a wide dirt road that appeared to be well traveled. Across the street was a unique and interesting looking masonry villa surrounded by a few small trees and vegetation. It had two stories, and attached to one side was an open porch with a three-foot-high wall of stone on all sides, affording the one time occupant a little privacy. It could have been used for sleeping in the hot evening summer or for sunbathing, but, perhaps more likely, for entertaining, as the villa was within walking distance of the well-known Michelin Rubber Plantation, producer of rubber products and tires. Because of its moderate size I assumed it housed a caretaker at one time. Sadly, the abandoned house was without doors and windows, and, unfortunately, its once fine architecture was heavily pockmarked with bullet holes.

Staring at the house, I began to wonder about the enemy. When I encountered him, how would I react? Would I be capable of doing the things I was trained to do? Suddenly someone sitting on a bunker about sixty feet behind me shouted out, "You're either on a suicide mission or you're one of the FNGs."

"Excuse me," I yelled back.

"You're standing in front of my bunker. You're in my field of fire. And you're nearly standing on top of my garden of claymores" (land mines). "Unless you want to be a statistic, I suggest you stay behind the bunkers."

Feeling foolish and wondering when I would be free of my new label, I stalked off.

Around noontime and feeling a little hungry, I headed over to the mess tent. I searched around in hopes of spotting John or Pete, Roger or Miles Touchberry, the medic, to sit with. Even Green would do, but to no avail. The only familiar faces I saw were two of the guys I had come in with yesterday and were assigned to other companies. I decided to join them. We said our hellos and immediately began comparing notes. I was surprised to learn both of them would be going out on night ambush tomorrow.

"The company lost four men last week," said one of the new recruits. What disturbed me even more was learning most of the others who had come in with us were already out on daytime missions. After speaking with John, I thought perhaps there would be a little down time to adjust to the new surroundings before getting into the thick of it. Shortly after lunch I heard my company had returned from their ambush mission and were coming in through the wire. I remember getting my canteen and walking over to the water wagon to fill it. There, from a distance, I was able to get a glance at these returning warriors who would be my companions, my partners and my support for the next three hundred and sixty some odd days. For a moment, I speculated as to which one of these soldiers would watch my back. I never envisioned it would be the company commander.

I watched the men one by one as they entered the campgrounds. The first thing I noticed was the jungle fatigues they were wearing were identical to mine, minus the starch and creases. Their fatigues were covered with dirt and mud and looked as though they'd been lived in for quite some time. Their faces appeared as if they had been in the center of a dust storm. They walked in single file formation, and from what I could hear from their conversations, they were elated to be back. Their spirits were high and their jokes morbid and off-color, were abundant.

"Hope that Gook had life insurance," someone yelled out.

"He's got more metal in him than a Sherman tank," shouted another. I could hear orders being called to fall out, dismissing the group with an added reminder that a roll call for guard duty and night LP's (listening posts) would be taken at 1700 hours.

"All are invited and you too may be a winner," one of the platoon leaders sarcastically called out.

Returning to my company area, I was quick to be spotted and heckled by several of the seasoned troops.

"FNG, FNG," called one.

"Fresh meat," called another.

"Hey, thank God my replacement is here and I can finally get off line. Thank you God."

"Yeah right, Mosley, how many weeks have you been here?" And on and on until the first sergeant stepped in and introduced me to the company. Over the remaining hours up until roll call, I met most of the men from my 3rd platoon and a good number from the other platoons. Some were cool. Some were funny. A couple of them were obnoxious. And then there were those noticeably few that, for reasons I failed to fully understand at the time, stayed away and avoided me altogether. They were the ones who recently lost a buddy or a partner and the best and only way they could handle it was by avoiding unnecessary new contacts and by shutting people out. They were the unfortunate ones who were transported beyond an imaginary line and depleted of feelings such as simplicity and innocence.

There was lots of chitchat, handshaking, pats on the back and a salute or two. I was focused on discovering someone I could connect to — New York, Cape Cod, Yonkers, Truro, Nebraska (where I did a season in college), Florida (where I worked towards a degree in architecture), Irish, whatever. So much was coming down so fast I just needed to relate to someone. To something. Anything. Not much more than 72 hours ago I was in Yonkers. Now I was in what was referred to as no-man's land.

By 5 PM the high spirits I had witnessed in the men earlier changed to one of apprehension as a sprinkling of the 3rd platoon began to gather near and around the company command bunker in anticipation of the reading of the night's assignments. Soon after, Gramps showed up with a clipboard in hand. The first sergeant, holding a cup of coffee in one hand, a lit cigarette in the other, was seated on a nearby bunker.

"Okay 3rd platoon, listen up," Sergeant Risley called out as he lit a cigarette. "We have four bunkers to cover on this fine night." As he read off about a dozen names, oddly a sigh of relief could be heard from those who were called. I thought that to be curious. Leaning over to one of the men who had saluted me earlier, I inquired, "Is guard duty a good thing?"

"It ain't so much that," he responded, "as much as it is they won't be called for LP tonight." LP, I thought. That's when you're sent out beyond the protection of the wire and into the camouflage of night, several hundred feet distant from the camp, where you sit absolutely still near a pathway and wait quietly for the approaching enemy. Its purpose was to give an early warning and advance notice to the base camp. A dangerous and often terrifying assignment and not particularly popular with the men.

"Okay, okay, okay," Sergeant Risley said as he continued on. "Tonight's LP will consist of Jenkins, Phillips and Gecko." To which Jenkins called out, "Come on Gramps, I pulled LP the night before we went out on patrol."

"That's a negative," the sergeant retorted, calling out the three names he had on his list for the last LP, Jenkins not being one of them. Abruptly, one of the guys I met yesterday who stayed behind called out, "That's affirm, Sarge. Jenkins took my place after I cut my foot on some broken glass."

"Right," said the sergeant. "Okay, so we're one shy. Do I have any volunteers?" he added. There was silence. The men were doing whatever was necessary to avoid eye contact.

"What about you, Williams?" the sergeant yelled.

"Got KP tomorrow," Williams responded, then added, "What about the new guy?" The sergeant, glancing over in my direction seemed to be giving me the once-over. He took a long drag on his cigarette. As I sat on the nearby bunker I must have looked as if I just walked out of a dry cleaners. Surely he's not going to call me, I thought. He then turned to the first sergeant. There was a lengthy pause. No words were exchanged. Eye contact by the men was now trained on me. Top was now looking down at his cup of coffee. The sergeant tossed his half-smoked cigarette to the ground.

"Phillips, Gecko and McCormick. Be here with your gear nineteen thirty sharp," the sergeant shouted out. The men of the 3rd platoon began to break up as they scattered in all directions.

"That's 7:30 tonight in human speak," John Paxson said, seemingly to have appeared out of nowhere. Placing his arm around my shoulders he continued, "Keep your chin up, kid, and come with me. I'll get you through this evening." With tension building from within, I accompanied John over to the company command center where he took me inside. Except for the two of us, it was empty. It was not a particularly large bunker, but you could stand up and there was enough space for a few people to move around. It had electricity that powered a mini refrigerator, two fans, and several light bulbs that were suspended from the metal reinforced ceiling. Besides the two radiotelephones, there were a couple of rickety old chairs and a small wooden table shared by Top and the captain. There were also three cots. John's was one of them and was located away from the other two in a sort of L-shaped area.

He had two poncho liners hanging, one in front and the other to the side to provide him a bit of privacy. He told me to sit as he grabbed a small trunk from under his cot. From it he pulled two packets of instant tea, a can of pineapple bits, a can of pound cake and a poncho liner which he handed to me with the following advice.

"This should make the evening go by quicker. Ask for first watch. Should you make contact with the enemy, do what you have to do, then call in and request permission to return to the base camp. That's important. Do you hear me? You don't want to stay out there after a shootout. If anyone argues with you about returning before sunup, you say to whoever is taking the call that you are at a tactical disadvantage since your location has been exposed to the enemy. Got that? You'll do okay."

Top entered the bunker. Alongside of him was the company CO. Introductions were brief as the captain focused on a map that Top was spreading out on his cot. Feeling in the way, I thanked John for his gifts and advice and left.

Maybe it was because I was new. Maybe it was because I was a bit frightened. Or maybe it was just the good manners my mother instilled in me. Whatever the reason, I appeared almost thirty minutes early for LP and my very first assignment beyond the wire. I waited by the gate for the other two as the sunlight faded slowly in the distance. The camp was quieting down. I looked around to re-acclimate myself to the camp's interior and at the same time wondered what would happen to me if I had to make a run for the gate in the middle of the night. Would one of our people mistake me for the enemy?

To my left and right were soldiers sitting on top of bunkers. In front of every other bunker was a stationary M-60 machine gun. Two men strolled by me carrying large bazooka-like weapons. Passing them was another soldier holding metal ammunition containers in each hand. Beyond him were four men tossing a football, back and forth.

At 7:30 PM, both guys showed up. Phillips, carrying the radio, introduced himself and then introduced me to Gecko. "We call Gecko 'Geek' 'cause he's a Geek, right Geek?" Phillips said, ribbing Gecko. Actually with the glasses he wore and the pens sticking out of his pocket he did sort of look like one. Besides, he had two knapsacks. We talked a bit trying to get to know each other. Phillips, though non-threatening, was the quintessence of macho. It only took a moment for me to realize he was one of the four playing touch football though I do not recall ever seeing him connect with a pass.

This was Phillips's third month in country but he came across as if he had been born and raised here. He had approximately ninety days more time than I did, so I felt I needed to pay attention. He said he heard we had the villa tonight and, if so, that's a real bummer. He said you had to use your ears more than your sight, because the villa had a three-foot-high wall around the upstairs porch where you sat your post, and it was an annoyance to keep popping your head up over it checking for Charlie. He began to describe the villa in detail. I was becoming more concerned, as the possibility of going out on LP with not one but two geeks was very real indeed, since the villa Phillips was describing was the one a few hundred feet across the road and plainly visible. As he rambled on, Gramps showed up again with clipboard in hand.

"Everyone all right?" he inquired, as he pulled a pencil from behind his ear and scribbled something on his pad. I was thinking, shouldn't that be a question asked tomorrow? He continued with his queries, wanting to know if we had a back-up battery for the radio, a supply of ammunition and insect repellant. (On the surface he seemed tense and less at ease than earlier at roll call.) He described reports by some of the local villagers of enemy movement over the past few nights. He lit a cigarette, cautiously cupping his hands to mask the flame and continued, saying some of this activity was taking place along the pathways behind the villa. Taking a good long drag and looking over his shoulders as though someone was watching him, he added we should be on our toes and cautioned us to be extra alert tonight. I started to get a sinking feeling in the pit of my stomach. I wanted so badly to ask, shouldn't you be sending someone else with more experience than I? For a moment or two there was complete silence as the three others stared across the roadway towards the villa. Evidently the sergeant was waiting for the sun to set completely before sending us out beyond the wire and across the road.

The villa, that seemed so attractive and inviting in the daylight hours, had now begun to take on a more menacing appearance. With each passing minute, the empty shell of the interior grew darker and darker. How do we know someone isn't in there already, I thought? It was then that Phillips called out, "Let's move." The sergeant stepped forward and unhooked the hardware that secured the gate to the wire. With the help of Phillips, he tugged it back, creating a few feet of clearance that allowed us to cross over. I didn't know the exact time but it was on the shy side of being totally dark as the three of us left behind our campsite and crossed the dirt road heading in the direction of our Listening Post.

Within a few minutes we were at the front entrance. Phillips was leading the way, Gecko was behind him and I followed. Having pulled this assignment before, he led the way taking us through the open door then right to the L-shaped stone staircase that led to the second floor. From there, using a penlight he carried along with his gear, Gecko cast a narrow beam of light that guided us along a wooden planked corridor and up to a door that opened to the outside veranda. The total darkness accompanying us throughout the house melted away as the three of us moved outside onto the deck and under the glow of the evening stars. The first thing Phillips did was to set up the radio and call into the command center to alert them we were in place. This was important, he told me, for if the camp came under attack, we did not want any of our people firing at the villa as had happened in the past. The second thing he did was to go off in a corner, unbutton his fly, lean over the side and take a long leak.

"It's a ritual of his," whispered Gecko. "He's hoping that the enemy is walking by and gets a sample of how he feels about them."

By 9 we had reviewed radio procedures and set up watch assignments. I requested and was given the first three-hour shift, which started at 9. We familiarized ourselves with the layout of the deck. In the far-left corner where I sat was a small wooden trap door. I lifted it when I first arrived and discovered it opened onto a terrace below. We also checked the exterior parameters, surreptitiously peeking over the three-foot-high wall every few minutes. As we sat there in silence, the two of them gradually allowed the war to go away. Phillips spoke of home and friends and girls and football. Gecko talked about an R&R (Rest and Recreation) he would soon be taking and how he would like to get his pilot license one day even though the Air Force wouldn't consider him for any of their fly programs since he wore glasses. I spoke about Westchester and my old neighborhood and my neighbors the Graniers and the DeGregorios and that we never had to lock our doors even when we went away (we never had a key). I also spoke of New York and its glamour and the Broadway shows I attended. I was a bit disappointed neither of them were familiar with "Hello Dolly," which I had seen five times.

"I'd take a game at Yankee Stadium anytime over a Broadway show," commented Phillips.

"You haven't seen anything till you witness an air show like I did at the Hanscom Air Force Base in Bedford, Mass." said Gecko. We spoke for some time and, although our conversation appeared innocent and non-challenging, none of us even for a moment were without doubts as to the potential perils that lurked about.

By 10 o'clock we were feeling a bit more relaxed. Above hushed whispers, I even poked a little fun at Phillips and suggested there was more to life than football and girls. I think he liked my style to the degree I got him to laugh at himself and not take himself so seriously. The macho façade and impression of self-importance portrayed earlier was slowly fading. He even referred to me by my first name on a few occasions. Meanwhile, Gecko and I debated the unfairness of not being able to fly for the Air Force if you wore prescription glasses. What's the big deal, we figured? If you drop or lose a pair, have another one with you.

Curious as to the strength of his prescription I asked for and received permission to try on his glasses, which appeared to be thicker than average. He handed them over to me. Wearing them for a few moments, even in the dimness of night made me feel a touch light-headed. Looking over at Phillips sitting in the far corner, I could see him, with blurred vision, giving me the finger. It seemed he was regressing from the camaraderie we shared earlier. It figures, I thought. No hope for him. Playing along, I raised both of my hands outward, mimicking a blind person.

It was then that Gecko leaned over and slapped his hand across my face at the same time pulling his glasses off of me. I was totally caught off guard as Gecko continued to squeeze one hand tightly around my mouth. Attempting to pull his hand off and at the same time looking across the terrace, I was stunned to see Phillips was not giving me the finger, but, in fact, had a finger stretched out and upward in front of his lips. He cautioned me to be quiet. His other hand was stretched far out in front with palm open, indicating for us to stop what we were doing. It was only a matter of seconds before I realized something was very wrong. The smell of cigarette smoke permeated the air around us. Gecko, ever so slowly, removed his hand from around my mouth, adjusted his glasses, grabbed his weapon and whispered one word, "Gooks."

Phillips, with slow and mechanical movements, stretched over to the radio and turned the volume down several notches to less than a whisper. He then removed his helmet. Getting up on his knees and with his back to us, he cautiously peeked over the side. The stars gave out more than enough light to see whatever might be out there. It seemed like an eternity as he stared out into the tree-lined fields that surrounded the back of the villa. Slowly he sat back down, waving his hands and nodding his head, indicating that he could see nothing from his side of the porch.

Sitting directly alongside Gecko, it was now our turn to check our side. Gecko, without hesitation and without removing his helmet, placed both hands on top of the wall. Cautiously he pulled himself up to the top and glanced over. He immediately pushed back and away from the wall and held up his hand with one finger extended and pointed down below. Phillips quietly moved over next to us.

"What did you see?" inquired Phillips.

"One Gook," Gecko responded. "He's standing below us on the lower terrace smoking a cigarette. He's checking out the base camp. Just staring. Didn't see anyone else, but there could be more."

"Weapons?" Phillips asked.

"Didn't see one," said Gecko. Phillips grabbed the radio handset and squeezed the key once, twice, three times, alerting the command center that we had contact with the enemy and they were too close to us for any type of verbal communication. Phillips then whispered, "We have to off him," indicating we had to kill him. "McCormick, you're the FNG, you're gonna open the trap door and frag him. Got that?" He wanted me to drop a hand grenade.

Only moments earlier Phillips was on a first name basis with me. He knew I was from Yonkers. He knew I attended a private school. He knew a lot about me in the short period of time we'd been together. Now I was reduced to a Fuck'n New Guy.

"I don't have any grenades," I whispered back.

"What?" Phillips exclaimed, whispering in tones a higher level than before. "What the fuck you mean you don't have any grenades? Jesus Christ!"

I asked him for one of his. He told me his assignment was to carry the radio and not grenades. Then he added, "Damn! What about you, Gecko?"

Lifting one of his two knapsacks and peeling back the flap, Gecko displayed an arsenal consisting of at least a dozen hand grenades. "Motherfuck! You don't travel light!" Phillips murmured. Gecko swiftly passed two of the grenades over to me. I couldn't believe the position I was placed in. I was actually in the process of taking a human life. I laid the first grenade down in my lap and held the other with my hand tightly clasped around the release lever. As I was taught in Advanced Infantry Training, I bent the safety pin forward and pulled it out. The grenade was now armed. At that moment I had two things on my mind. One, once the lever was released, I would have less than ten seconds to get rid of the grenade without blowing the three of us up. Two, there would be no need for me to go to the latrine anytime soon.

"You okay?" I didn't know who asked that.

"I'm okay."

"You ready?" Gecko asked.

I nodded my head. Ever so slowly, Gecko lifted the trap door, just an inch at a time until there was enough clearance for me to drop the grenade. I didn't like what I was doing, but I was trained to do this. I also wanted to get rid it. Everything was now set. No reason existed for me not to follow through. I leaned forward, which now allowed me for the first time to get a good look at my adversary.

Leaning up against the outside wall of the villa stood a young man of medium build. He wore dark trousers and a long-sleeved tan shirt. He was wearing sandals and his feet were crossed. A lit cigarette was moving from hand to mouth. So far he hadn't a clue there were three additional souls who were not much more than a few yards away and who had already made the decision to end his life. I wanted to ask, "Is this our enemy?" but I knew this was not the time. This was not the place. Besides, Gecko labeled him and he had the experience. I let go of the lever and dropped the hand grenade. Gecko quickly closed the hatch door creating a noise louder than was necessary. Immediately, the sound of the metal object hitting the lower concrete floor, bouncing once or twice, echoed all around us. A rustling sound could be heard from below, then seconds later the explosion. This was immediately followed by the sounds of an M-16 being fired from inside the base camp.

Phillips quickly stood up in a semi-crouched position. He pointed his rifle outward while he examined the surrounding area. It was deadly silent. From across the road and inside the base camp a voice, barely audible, could be heard calling out, "You Goddamn Gooks, we're ready for you." We decided to open the hatch. As I lifted it, Gecko, already with penlight in hand, cast a narrow beam of light down below. Our visitor was nowhere to be seen. Phillips told us to keep a sharp lookout on all sides as he called the command center and asked permission to return. The response was a negative one as the officer on duty stated it was only 22:30. (10:30)

"Tell them that our LP has been compromised since the enemy is now aware of our location," I said to Phillips.

"Yeah. Right! I like that, McCormick," he replied back.

"Also tell them we no longer have the tactical advantage and that our safety is at risk," I added.

"Man that's fuck'n good. You should be on the radio," Phillips commented. After a brief discussion between Phillips and the command center, permission to return was granted. We packed up our gear and made our way down and through the dark interior and then outside. Phillips wanted to first inspect the lower veranda to see if there were any signs of our visitor. We found no one. Gecko threw a narrow beam of light, first on the floor, then on the wall. Splotches of blood could be seen over a large area. Our visitor had been hit. The question was, how far did he go and where had he gone?

Once we were back we were debriefed. A young lieutenant, who appeared as if he just awoke, hit us up with a salvo of questions. Another looking quite a bit older joined in: "What direction was he looking? Was he taking notes? How was he dressed? Did we see others?" The time was now a little after midnight. Upon completion of the interrogation, we were allowed to return to our company. As we stood up to exit, the cries of "incoming" could be heard from several different directions outside the bunker as the first of a barrage of enemy mortar rounds began to fall on our base camp. From our perspective it seemed the majority of the exploding mortars were landing in and around the mess tent. "Damn! What did the cook make for dinner tonight?" an officer joked as he peeked around the sandbag entranceway. This was my very first experience of being under fire. Oddly, I felt relatively at ease and somewhat secure. Perhaps it had something to do with being inside this well-fortified bunker. Or maybe it had something to do with the fact I was around a number of people a lot more experienced than I who did not seem to get all that excited about what was happening. After only a minute or two the sounds of the exploding mortars came to a stop.

I soon realized our nighttime visitor was doing more than just sightseeing. In all probability, he was a local villager and farmer by day, an enemy sympathizer with the role of "spotter" by night, with the responsibility of closely watching camp activity, pinpointing targets, then passing this along to the nearby enemy. Only a few hours earlier I was questioning who the enemy was. I was debating whether or not I was justified in taking a life that appeared to be little or no threat to me.

Later, I sat outside a bunker alone for the remainder of that evening. I was contemplating how things might have turned out if I had reacted differently or perhaps not at all. The enemy was without a face, I was thinking. Whom do we trust and when do we not? But that was not my foremost concern. I wondered what might become of me should I fail to question who the enemy really was.

INNOCENCE LOST

December 1968

Dearest David,

Hope you are well and keeping your head down.
Saw Aunt Kay yesterday. She said that she had already
received three letters from you. Think she is back
on the bottle...the weather has been cold here and...

Love,

The Mother

PS – Walk on the sidewalk

History was never my forte. For the most part dates, no matter how historical, just did not interest me. The shooting of President Kennedy on November 22, 1963, yes, I did remember, perhaps because it was real history which had taken place in my lifetime. But, when it came to academics and recalling important dates that took place in world history, I could be counted as a failure. Even the significant date of December 7, 1941, the bombing of Pearl Harbor and our entrance into World War II, escaped my mind.

December 7, 1968 did, however, take on a special meaning for me. It became a date in my life that categorically changed me as I matured in a very short period of time. It was the day I was officially entitled to wear the CIB (Combat Infantryman's Badge). The badge is approximately 3 inches long and three-quarters-inch wide. It is blue in color and has a large oak-leaf cluster that encircles a Revolutionary War musket. The decorative medal is for infantry soldiers only. It is something awarded and worn more for distinction than honor. Although it is an honor to wear it, it is awarded for one purpose — to recognize the fact you actually engaged in battle and returned fire on

21

a hostile force. This day marked the first time in my life anyone had shot at me, and I had shot at someone.

On that day, while out on patrol, we walked into an ambush. I had been on line only a short period of time. The VC totaled no more than half a dozen in strength. Our company then consisted of approximately eighty men. The VC's only intention was to maim or kill one or more of our people. By doing so, they in turn would be recognized and honored by their people. When they opened up on us, their selected target was the 3rd platoon. My platoon. It was also where the captain, along with his RTO, John Paxson, had been walking at the time. Perhaps we were the targets because of the radio antennas. Everything happened so quickly as the captain shouted orders to get down and return fire. Our return volley was short but massive. Using my weapon for the first time I fired off close to an entire clip.

As the dust was settling there was shouting among the men, then a few moments of silence as the enemy seemed to just disappear. Soon after, Pete Arnone called over to John and asked if I had ever been in a firefight before.

"Hey, that's right, McCormick's no longer a virgin," John called out.

"Private McCormick, you have just entered the very elite CIB club," the captain called over to me. Since I was the newest recruit on line, it appeared as if everyone was staring at me. Checking me out. Looking to see how I reacted during my very first battle.

Since it was my first firefight, I think I did okay. However, any doubts I may have harbored about someone out there trying to harm me now completely dissipated. It was only a small battle, one I would later refer to as a "skirmish." But indeed, someone had in fact fired his weapon with the intention to cause injury. From start to finish the incident lasted no more than a minute. Whatever amount of bullets the enemy fired upon us paled compared to the amount of return fire we lodged back. Yet I remembered one bullet the enemy fired quite well and the sound of that bullet coming so close you can actually hear the reverberation it makes slicing through the air at super velocity. It was a sound I will never forget. It was also a sound I would hear again and again.

I soon learned this type of engagement with the enemy was commonplace. An entire company consisting in excess of 100 men can have their mission dramatically altered by just one or two snipers. Truly, it does not take much to stop or slow down the company. Although my first experience of engaging the enemy was a relatively minor one, there would be others. From a physical standpoint I survived this first firefight, and I handled it as well as can be expected. But bigger battles with larger enemy forces loomed ahead, where my mental ability would be put to the real test.

Besides being shot at, the month of December marked another discernable distinction for me. It was the very first time I carried the radiotelephone. John Paxson coaxed me into it, perhaps not without reason. During night ambush, when it was my turn to pull guard duty, there were several occasions when I communicated information to the command center. Most times John would be at the other end. The reports I called in ran the gamut from blasé (someone snoring or relieving himself), to apprehensive (enemy sightings). Through this period of time a trust and a bond developed between the two of us. John, it seemed, liked the way I handled myself and communicated on the radio during daytime operations and night ambush. Through the short period of time I carried the radio for the 3rd platoon, John, who was very much battle seasoned, gave me advice when necessary and counseling when needed. He was a good teacher who instinctively knew when to exercise patience and when not. Under fire, he remained calm. And after a battle his sense of humor, dry and dark and cryptic, went into overdrive.

John was good enough to keep an eye on me for the purposes of teaching and training, especially on the use and proper procedures of radio communication. I, in turn, was able to observe John in an up close and personal way. One thing I found most fascinating about him was his overall perception of the war. It was quite different from most others. John looked at the war as nothing more than an imposition. With John, a clash with the enemy was merely an incidental hostility. He took nothing personally. He also would not allow things to hinder his personal perspective of this land and its people. In non-combatant situations, he displayed a respect and admiration for the Asians that was uncanny. This included their culture and their food. The latter brought out many of John's culinary talents. When taking a break at one of the small villages in the middle of the jungle, it would not be unusual to find John conversing, in whatever communicable way possible, with any of the locals, especially the ones doing the day's cooking. John had a knack for this, and it seemed to be a talent. While out on riverboat missions, with all Vietnamese crews, John would conjure up tasty concoctions consisting of canned C-rations, small bits of fresh killed fish, mixed with a little rice on the side. It was suspected, but never confirmed, that John carried along his own personal seasonings. Without fail, the very young Vietnamese Navy crew would be in awe of him.

Towards the end of December, John, had first broached the subject of carrying the captain's radio. At the time I had little or no interest. Although I had participated in several enemy encounters, I was still new on line. Yet, from the beginning, I had become very attentive to the various activities and roles played during the course of a mission. With these observations in mind it took little imagination to realize one thing. Being around the captain, whose command group consisted of other officers and RTOs, with the obvious presence of tall antennas flapping about, made for an attractive target. It was not my idea of being in a safe environment. John was good enough not to push me in this area. He also allowed me the space needed to gather my own experiences with the handling of radio operations for the 3rd platoon.

As time moved along I learned the burden of carrying the radio was not just a physical one. Mentally you had to be there. I learned to develop a perception and feel for an assortment of situations. By doing so I was able to bond common sense with intuition. Whether a patrol or a firefight, if something didn't seem right or didn't appear to be going well, I would consult with my platoon leader. In turn the captain would be informed.

During this time period in December I clung closely to my new circle of friends. John Paxson, Pete Arnone, Miles Touchberry and Roger Wasson were never beyond shouting distance. Roger was from San Jose, California. We alternated carrying the radio and found we had much in common including a similar sense of humor. It seemed we both had a built-in safety mechanism that allowed us to ignore certain life and death situations and, in fact, at times even make light of it. This was a manageable immorality that helped us to cope with the day-to-day realities of a war and, at the same time, assisted us in maintaining our sanity. Roger was a very private person who allowed few people into his fold. I considered myself lucky, I became one of them.

Pete Arnone amused me with stories of New York and his upbringing in the Bronx. One thing I took note of about Pete was he took the war very seriously. He was also responsible for a good deal of the firepower that came out of any given confrontation with the enemy. Unfortunately, Pete would be the first in our group to be hit. His getting wounded would serve as a lesson about the ramifications of getting too close to anyone. For me, the month of December marked the first time in my life I witnessed death and dying. Up close. And personal.

The end of the month approached, and with multiple missions under my belt along with all I had experienced to date I felt I was as seasoned as I could be. But, as in all wars, new and different experiences are never more than a conflict away. En route to a suspected enemy camping ground, our company had taken a little detour. Not too far from our objective was a village consisting of several dozen huts and some large storage areas that contained rice. Captain Wong, was our new CO and recently took over command from Captain Larry Rubino. He was the ranking officer in charge of the company and wanted to see what information, if any, he could get from some of these villagers. If they were cooperative, that could be helpful. If not, that would be useful in knowing which side of the fence they sat on. It would also be the type of information that would be passed on to S-2 (intelligence) for future monitoring.

As we entered the village, one of the first things that struck Captain Wong as being out of place was the fact there were several boys in the age group of fourteen to sixteen-years-old. In addition there was a young man who was just standing around. This struck the captain as odd since the males were all within draft age. Orders were given to interrogate all villagers. Captain Wong compiled a series of questions and passed them on to our Vietnamese interpreter. But before any inquiries were made the captain had us separate the males from the females. Wong's 'thinking cap' was never in the off position. He wanted to see how the men would respond and compare their answers to those of the women.

For the most part, the young man and the boys had plausible excuses why they were not in the military. The boys said something about being from the far South. They had come to the village in search of relatives since both of their fathers had been killed while fighting in the war. Captain Wong, listening intently to the interpreter, quickly shot back, "Which side?" In unison, "South," was their reply. Truthful or well rehearsed? It was hard to say.

The young man responded in a similar way and seemed convincing. He said he had been shot and lifted his shirt to show the scar. The women, however, were an entirely different matter. But it wasn't the answers that bothered Captain Wong. It was the way they answered the questions. They were openly hostile to the interpreter and our troops and made no qualms about it. Captain Wong's intuitive suspicions were raised a notch. He did not like this one bit, but what could he do? Besides, we were under time constraints to reach our objective, and without any hard evidence it was difficult to say whether or not any of them were VC or were sympathetic to the enemy. Orders were given to continue our journey. We moved on.

As we exited the small village we were not more than a few hundred feet down the road when we took a round of sniper fire. Luckily no one was hit. However, with rice paddies on three sides of us that offered absolutely no cover, one thing was obvious. The fire had to have come from the village. Orders were given to return to the village and conduct a hut-by-hut search to seek out the sniper. This took about thirty minutes. We were as thorough as possible and yet turned up nothing. One thing was evident: the young man we interrogated earlier was conspicuously absent. Captain Wong, not a man to waste time, figured the sniper had gotten away and ordered us to continue on our mission. On the move once more and only a short distance from the village we took another round of sniper fire. Again, as with the previous shots, no one was hit. This second attack did not sit well with the captain.

After briefly consulting with his platoon leaders he ordered the village surrounded. No one in. No one out. For sure, this time the sniper would be trapped within the confines of the compound. Orders were given once more to enter the village and conduct a hut-by-hut search. Once again we came up empty-handed. With the entire village surrounded, the sniper had to be hiding somewhere inside. Wong was concerned if he exited the village again without locating the sniper, the next shot might take down one of his men.

But the captain was not one to play games with. He ordered the company to move on. This time however, he chose several men to stay behind and hide out in a few of the empty huts in anticipation of the sniper's return. I was one of the men.

"McCormick, you're on my frequency, you're gonna be my eyes and my ears and report to me on the slightest activity," the captain said as he and the remainder of the company exited the village. As the men moved out, John passed by me and offered the following advice: "Look, this is a great opportunity to show off your communication skills to the captain. Just call it as you see it, and report everything."

In a matter of minutes the remainder of the company could be seen marching away, while I, along with a few others from the 3rd platoon, remained hidden inside one of the grass and mud huts within the village. It was spooky in a way. As the company headed off, all the local villagers stayed in their huts. We sat and we waited. We also figured if the sniper was hiding nearby and wanted to fire more shots at our company he had only a short time frame to do this. Slowly the minutes ticked by. The pathways of the village remained empty. To say the least, nerves were on end. It was deathly quiet, almost too quiet for a village of this size. Something was not right. Something was up and the villagers knew enough to stay in their huts. Then it happened. The sniper who was nowhere to be found during our earlier searches just walked out of one of the huts not more than a hundred feet in front of us. Looking about and stretching briefly, he walked a short distance and now stood front and center of two of the huts that concealed members of our third platoon. I diligently relayed this to Captain Wong.

He was about five foot five inches and seemed as if he was in his late twenties or possibly early thirties. His facial features were hardened and he was darker skinned than most of the Vietnamese I had come in contact with to date. He was dressed in dark brown pants and wore a plain long sleeved shirt that was similar in color. Slung over his shoulder was an AK-47 assault rifle. He also seemed completely oblivious to our presence.

The enemy soldier couldn't have been standing there more than a few seconds when gunfire erupted from inside both of the huts. For the most part snipers were something you had little or no protection from. Oftentimes the success of their missions can be measured by the degree of their concealment. The sniper never knew what hit him and died the type of death he himself had perhaps meted out at another time.

With the soldier lying dead in the village, it was decided a message needed to be sent to the other villagers. That message was if you give shelter or refuge or support of any type to the enemy, then this would be the consequence. A rope was found and tied around the body. It was then dragged along the pathways that entwined the village, passing as many huts as we could, allowing as many villagers as possible to see the body.

Over the years, with all the happenings and events that went on while growing up in Yonkers, the month of December in the year 1968 was the period of time that brought radical and unconditional changes in my life, resulting from what I had seen and experienced and taken part in. These changes came from within. I grew. I developed. I aged. I crossed over that mystical time line that transforms you from boyhood to manhood. But there was also something else that took place during this period of time. It wasn't a change, but more so a realization of frightening proportions. It was the time in my life when I came to realize the odds of staying alive over here were not necessarily in my favor.

THE LONG GOOD NIGHT

January 1969

Dearest David,

Hope you are good and without injuries. Don't know if you heard, but your father has announced his plans to marry Suzanne.
The weather has been nice here and...

Love,

The Mother

PS – Walk on the sidewalk

I can't recall exactly what awakened me that night in 1955. It was one of those cold northeast December evenings just a few weeks before Christmas. The extra blankets that covered me more than made up for the chill in the room. The serenity I felt while lying in the comfort of my bed was short-lived and overshadowed by raised voices that came from the living room down below. It was around ten thirty. Sitting up in bed I could only guess my father had shown up and, as often the case, was arguing with my mother.

A quick trip to the window confirmed my suspicions. Sitting in front of the house and partially covered with a light dusting of snowflakes was my father's big black Chrysler Imperial. Seeing the car stirred a mixture of emotions from within. My father was not a warm or affectionate person (his love, devotion and true mistress was his business), and I cannot recall ever feeling the warmth of his touch or the security of a hug. What I do remember well at eight years of age was when he did make one of his rare appearances, and if you caught him in the right mood, he could mesmerize you with wonderful bedtime stories.

With this in mind I hurried to my door. Concerned that he was in one of his unpleasant moods, I cautiously tiptoed to the top of the stairs. Greeted with silence from below, I wondered whether he was reading the mail or, perhaps more likely, fixing a drink. Leaning against the banister and listening closely, I debated for a moment whether or not I should call down to him when, over the whisper of the outside winds, I thought I heard the sounds of an engine. Turning to my room I rushed back to my window only to discover an empty silhouette in place of his car. Tossing open the windows I fought back the cold evening air as I caught a glimpse of his car and the glow of the red taillights disappearing into the distance.

I wasn't sure what I wanted from my father that evening. Perhaps I just wanted him to read me a bedtime story. Or maybe I needed him to ask me how I was doing and for him to tell me to take care of myself. Possibly, I just wanted him to say good night to me. What I do know about that evening, is that I carried back to bed an overwhelming sense of loneliness and emptiness. On that December night I cried myself to sleep.

Those were my thoughts on this warm and humid night in 1969. It was a difficult twenty-four hours for me and the entire company. It had all started the day before when our company, on a search and destroy mission, was transported by helicopter and landed in what is referred to as a "Hot LZ" (landing zone under fire). I remember its being a large open field with some distance between our troops and the wood line that surrounded us. The moment we hit the ground we received enemy fire seemingly from every direction.

The high-pitched whining of the numerous huey helicopter engines all but muffled the popping sounds of the enemy AK-47 rifle fire and, within a matter of moments, four of our men were hit. One was hit in the hand, two others had arm wounds and a fourth had taken a bullet in the neck which somehow, miraculously, managed to miss all vital parts and appeared to be nothing more than a flesh wound. Although their injuries were not life threatening, I had the responsibility of calling in two medevacs (medical helicopters) while at the same time coordinating return fire with the assistance of the Cobra gunship that had accompanied us on our mission for that day.

After the dust settled and the wounded were removed, we received orders from the tactical command center back at headquarters to "stay" the ground and dig in. Thankfully, with the exception of a few harassing and misguided enemy mortar rounds, mingled with the shrieking sound of one of the new guys as he fought off his nightmares of war, the evening was uneventful.

The arrival of daylight brought new orders. Our mission was to stay where we were, create and fortify a perimeter and set up daily ambush sites in the hope of catching Charlie by surprise in broad daylight. We would be here one full week. These were the types of extended mini-missions everyone dreaded. Canned C-rations consisting of beans and franks, pineapple chunks and pound cakes were our daily staple. Showers were put on hold and sanitary conditions limited.

Captain Wong and the 3rd platoon leader, Lt. Sanchez spent most of the morning creating the list of supplies needed to sustain the troops and accomplish our objectives: from sandbags to barbed wire, to insect repellent and fresh water. In addition to C-rations, radio batteries and extra ammunition, we would call in for medical supplies, towels and toiletries. Lastly we would request trip wire for the enemy along with an assortment of candies from the Red Cross. By noontime, I had radioed in the completed list and, shortly after, the first of the many supply helicopters started to arrive.

It was a long, hot and exhausting day. Hauling the endless supplies from the wide-open fields to the sanctity of our wood line was grueling and tedious work. Whoever greeted us upon our arrival yesterday afternoon was nowhere to be found today. As the hours rolled on, a sense of calm engulfed the men. Possibly this sense of security was due to the numerous lift-offs and landings of the many helicopter supply ships. Possibly it was due to the deadly cobra gun-ship that occasionally would do a flyby. More likely though it was due to the unbearable heat of the day, along with the fact that, thankfully, for the moment, we were not being shot at.

I remember seeing two of the more seasoned men walking out to the middle of the open field without their weapons. A short distance away, one of the new guys, who had stripped down to his shorts, was taking a leak in the brush. Don't ever drop your guard, I thought.

The last shipment, which should have been the first, was the three boxed rolls of barbed wire. This was too heavy to have been brought out on one of the hueys (helicopters) and was en route to us by way of a Chinook, the long twin engine helicopter that was the workhorse of this war. It had enormous capacity to ferry supplies in and out. Affectionately, it was referred to by its pilots as "muleskinner" and not so affectionately by the men as a "shithook."

With the radio on my back and rifle in hand, accompanied by two other riflemen for security, I headed out into the open field to guide in the last of the supply ships for the evening. It was about 7:30 PM and I was anxious to get this supply drop over and return to our day-old campsite. (It's late, it's late, and Charlie moves at eight.) Because of the hour, and for the safety of our men, the barbed wire once dropped would stay out in the field until morning.

Off in the distance, the faint but distinctive sound of the twin engine helicopter could be heard but not seen. Instinctively I called out to the pilot on my radio using Captain Wong's call sign of "Charlie Papa" for Command Post.

"Muleskinner, muleskinner, this is Charlie Papa, do you read? Over," I called. Silence. I repeated, "Muleskinner, this is Charlie Papa, this is Charlie Papa, do you read? Over." Again, silence, except for the increasing sound of the engines.

A moment later, the airwaves crackled. "Charlie Papa, this is muleskinner, do you read me, over?"

"That's affirmative muleskinner, loud and clear, over," I responded.

"I roger that, Charlie Papa. What is your location? Over."

One of the few things of the war I took a little satisfaction in was being able to direct the landing of helicopters in the dark of night without giving out our exact grid location over the airwaves. I had my own system. I thought, if I repeated the grids exactly where we were located, it would give the enemy an extra edge if he were listening in.

"Muleskinner, this is Charlie Papa, flash your landing lights on and off for me, over."

With darkness upon us and no additional questions asked, I could see off in the distance, the soft glow of the landing lights as they flickered their response.

"Muleskinner, this is Charlie Papa, thank you for that, be advised that you are approximately three to four miles to our south and slightly to our right, do you copy? Over."

32

"Charlie Papa, we copy that. Is the LZ secured?" A prime question and one that no helicopter pilot fails to ask is whether or not his landing zone is safe or under fire. I informed him that, at the moment, the area was safe.

He had a very pleasing voice, which somehow comforted me. I assumed he was in his early to mid, 50's. As the sound of the engines got louder, I began to make out the sight of his flashing red strobe lights. While I waited patiently on the ground the pilot radioed out asking me where I was from.

"New York," I said, "well, actually a little north of the city, Yonkers, Yonkers, New York, ever hear of it?"

I threw the switch on the flashing strobe light and held it high. Guardedly the riflemen, now in a crouched position, were scrutinizing the surrounding fields.

"Affirmative," he said (again a long pause), "and thank y'all, we've got your strobe in sight."

Standing there in the wide-open field, we waited as the approaching Chinook, with our cargo box suspended from underneath, began its descent towards us.

"So, Charlie Papa," the pilot continued, "do you have a name?"

At this point the winds began to whip up and the ground to vibrate as the twin rotor blades, from this enormous flying machine, inched its way towards us. The sound from the two engines was deafening as it now hovered only a few feet above. The red flashing beacon lights cast an eerie glow on the faces of the men.

"DAVE!" I shouted into the handset, figuring with the reverberation of the engines there was no way on this planet he could possibly hear me.

Ever so gently the pilot lowered the over-sized crate that contained our barbed wire, just a foot at a time, then inch by inch until it was safely on the ground. I remember looking up at my radio antenna and thinking if it were another few inches taller it would be scraping the bottom of this big brown mechanical bird, and new antennas, out here in the field, were in short supply. I stepped back a few feet.

With our cargo safely on the ground the support hook was released. Backing away along with the other two riflemen, I raised my arm high in the air as I gave a 'thumbs-up' to the pilots, letting them know their mission was accomplished and they were clear to ascend. With a minimum of dignity and without much grace, this over-sized and awkward appearing flying machine began to slowly back away stirring up dirt and sand and grass from all directions. As the helicopter was now fully aloft and the thunderous sound of the engines receding, a sense of calm set in as the three of us made our way back to the wood line.

It could have been any number of things that triggered my mind into drifting that evening. It may have come from the overpowering quietness left with us by the recently departed supply copters. Or, it may have come from the dismal thoughts of having to spend a week out here in the field. Without showers. Without a hot cooked meal. Without a good night's sleep. Without knowing whether or not this was it. Your time was up. On this particular mission you would not be returning.

Whatever I felt snuck up on me and hit me like a ton of bricks. I felt very much alone and completely isolated on our journey back to our campsite. A sense of depression weighed heavily with each step. As my mind began to wander, I thought back to that cold December night in 1955.

I wondered if I should have called downstairs to my father that evening, to let him know I was awake. Had I not tiptoed so quietly from my room that night, perhaps he would have heard me and come up and told me a bedtime story. I wondered, should I have just called out and told him I needed him? This despair I now felt so consumed me, I wondered if I would make it back to the wood line.

Continuing on and approaching our campsite, the silhouettes of the men sitting guard duty slowly came into focus. With darkness now upon us I radioed in to reconfirm and alert anyone who was not aware that friendlies (we) were approaching. The only response from whoever was sitting guard duty was a simple and direct, "I roger that," meaning, hopefully, they were aware we were coming in and would not shoot at us.

With less than one hundred feet remaining between us and the wood line, the evening's silence was broken by the crackle of a radio transmission. Not having the handset to my ear and failing to hear the message, I quietly radioed back.

"This is Charlie Papa. Please say again, over." My transmission was met by silence. After a moment, I repeated: "This is Charlie Papa, this is Charlie Papa. Who's calling, over?"

"Roger, Charlie Papa, this is muleskinner, you still there, over?" came the response.

Surprised to hear from the helicopter pilot again, I couldn't help being a little amused he might think I could be anywhere else than on the ground. I was also very curious why he would have a reason to break the silence of the evening airwaves. I radioed back: "That's affirmative, muleskinner. What can I do for you? Over." I whispered.

No response. I could tell by his last transmission that his signal was growing weak and I might not hear from him again.

I repeated, "Muleskinner, muleskinner, this is Charlie Papa, did you forget something, over?"

With the distinctive sound of the southern voice along with the background hum of the twin engines, the silence of the airwaves broke once again.

"Dave, this is muleskinner."

His transmission was barely audible and somewhat broken up. I was so very touched by the fact he remembered and called me by name. He continued.

"Just wanted to tell ya'll to take real good care of yourself down there and you have a safe night, you hear me, son?"

Slowing my pace ever so slightly, I radioed back to him.

"Thanks. Thanks for the thought, muleskinner. And a good night to you, too."

His kind words had taken my fragile spirit and lifted it to heights I had not thought possible. Looking behind me and upwards, with tears in my eyes as I watched the faint glow of the red beacon lights fading off in the distance, I thought of my father and that cold winter night in 1955.

David William McCormick

RIVERBOAT OPERATION, THE FIRST 24 HOURS

February 1969

Dearest David,

*Got a nice letter from your cousin Bill Lennox. He's an Air
Force colonel stationed in Saigon and he asked your father
for your address. His son Billy was your partner when you
were Confirmed at Christ the King Church.*
*Got two letters from you today. Did I ever tell you Danny
the postman always rings the doorbell when he delivers a
letter from you?*

Been cold with snow on the way ...

Love,

The Mother

PS –Walk on the sidewalk

It was my third day without a shower. The sun was strong, the
temperature unforgiving. Rarely was it below 100 degrees. We were
on a search and destroy mission. It was a relatively quiet one with
very little action and, as yet, no sign or encounter with enemy troops.
Days such as this could easily lull you into a false sense of security.
Then, suddenly, you're caught off guard and without warning you get
attacked and you wonder, where the hell was I and what was I
thinking of, or why wasn't I focused on that tree or bush where the
gunfire came from? It gets especially bad and the guilt gets
compounded when it is your friend or buddy taking the hit. As much
as the enemy, complacency was something that had to be reckoned
with. As the day went by, we continued our hunt. A bit later on in
mid-afternoon I came across a dead deer lying in an open field. It
appeared to have been hit by shrapnel from a misguided or practice

round of artillery. As I walked by it, I was reminded the casualties of war were not just human ones. Staring into the glazed-over eyes I felt sorry for her and thought she had just been in the wrong place at the wrong time.

Around 11 AM on the fourth day I received a call for Captain Wong. It was from the Tactical Operations Command (TOC) center. "Charlie" was creating problems along a certain section of the Delta River. Apparently, the enemy was taking pot shots (and brazen enough to do this in broad daylight) at the riverboat crews that patrolled the area. Special orders were issued. Our unit was to hookup and work with the Navy riverboat patrol. It was to be a five-day mission and a welcome change of pace from the constant day-to-day struggles that occur in jungle warfare.

The men were elated with the prospect of this new venture. In addition our entire company was to be given a twenty-four hour stand-down in the neighboring town of Dau Tieng, twenty miles east of our location. Showers, clean jungle fatigues, fresh cooked food and, above all, freedom for the night awaited us.

The evening gave us choices. We could take in an outdoor movie or go for a swim in the town's pool. We could shop for things at the local PX like extra batteries for our personal radios, additional pairs of socks, sunglasses and underwear. We could load up on normal (non C-ration) foods and snacks to be enjoyed while out in the field.

There were other ways to elude the constant and hazardous daily realities we faced. One was extra sack time. Another was downing cold beers at the local hangout. Many opted for the latter. It wasn't so much for the beer, but for the companionship and camaraderie. Our infantry unit had a reputation. We went by the name of "The Wolfhounds" and when we visited towns such as Dau Tieng we were often treated as local heroes returning from a quest from some far-away conflict. Some of the camp support staff, which was made up of cooks and clerks, supply and medical personnel, would often be generous and quick to buy us a round or more of drinks. In return, someone would tell a story or two about coming face-to-face with the enemy. I opted to relax by taking a swim with some of the guys and, if only for a moment, search out and be a part of a piece of civilized normality in the center of a war so very far away from home. The days of youthful innocence and fun I so enjoyed while growing up

37

and hanging out at the Amacassin Swim and Tennis Club in Yonkers, New York, did not seem that long ago.

It was a bit after 3 PM when the convoy arrived to pick us up. A number of heavily armed jeeps, all of which had M-60 machine guns attached to the back, accompanied the vehicles. The drive into town was a long and rough one. A farmer or two could be seen off in the distance tending to their water buffaloes. Mama-sans, along with their young daughters, were working in the rice fields. We were escorted over bumpy dirt roads that were pockmarked with numerous craters both large and small, all compliments of the enemy and their road mines. Our trucks were open and uncovered and seemed to encourage the dust and the dirt that settled down upon us.

When we reached the town our convoy was stopped for inspection. Approaching the first truck at the gates, a military police sergeant ordered the men to remove their ammo clips and eject the rounds of ammunition locked in the chamber of the weapon. Apparently there had been a number of accidents and SIWs (self-inflicted wounds) lately, and the camp commander felt something had to be done to minimize this. This was the first time anything like this had happened to me and I was not about to make a big deal of it. After all, I had other things on my mind, among them, a long cool shower and relaxation at the pool.

The night and the activities seemed to come and go in an instant, and by early morning we were being airlifted out to the river. Once on the ground, we were divided up by platoons and then divided up again as the riverboats, along with their crews, had space limitations and could only accommodate a certain number of men per boat. Captain Wong, along with his lieutenants, met with and was briefed by the Navy's group commander.

It was immediately apparent these boats were not crewed by our Navy. Although the boats were ours, the crew was all South Vietnamese. The commander was an American Navy officer who spoke Vietnamese. His sole purpose was to work with and train these crews should technical or tactical questions arise. Whatever emotions I had previously felt regarding the excitement of being part of and working with the Navy completely diminished. It was common knowledge that the South Vietnamese Army was inadequately trained, poorly motivated and had very little discipline. I had no reason to think the South Vietnamese Navy differed in any way. Add to that the language barrier and you had the ingredients for extremely precarious conditions.

Our mission was to conduct daily sweeps along and inside the banks lining the river. We were to search out any signs of enemy presence such as campfires or leftover particles of food, footprints or human waste. We were to look for anything that might establish a pattern of activity around the area of the river. On the boat, I had set up the captain's radio alongside the South Vietnamese radio communications center. The boats were similar in size and shape to World War II PTs. Space was tight and somewhat restricted, but I wanted to make sure that Captain Wong had whatever was needed should problems arise. The commander introduced me to his South Vietnamese communications person whose English was understandable. I explained to him I was the radiotelephone operator with the company. I asked what frequency he used and gave him ours so we could keep in touch if and when we made enemy contact. He introduced me to the boat's RTO who either spoke no English or was very shy. He wore a red-checkered bandanna around his neck, had a constant smile and seemed to bow a lot.

Later that evening I spread out my poncho liner in a spot near the communication center. In anticipation of the next day's mission, I attempted to get some rest. All of the boats were lined up in a row. Our boat was facing the riverbank. For tactical purposes every other boat was positioned outward towards the opposite riverbank. Two men LPs (listening posts) were established on the banks approximately one to two hundred feet inland. They were all South Vietnamese Navy.

Around 11 P.M I needed to take a leak. Earlier we were cautioned by the commander to keep noise at an absolute minimum and to maintain a mode of silence throughout the evening. "Charlie" was looking for us and we did not want to become an easy target. As I gingerly made my way to the back of the boat I noticed what a beautiful night it was. The moon radiated as far down the river as I could see. The stars glimmered magnificently, and aside from the gentle sound of the waves stirring about the sides of the boat, there was absolute silence. After what seemed to be an eternity, I finished my business, headed back to my area where I lay down and covered my head with my poncho liner.

The next morning as we geared up to head out for the day's sweep, I decided to cap off my canteen with water from the river. As I leaned over the side I saw a body floating by me down the river. Dressed in the traditional black outfit that was commonly worn by the enemy VC, he was floating face up. His bloated body created an eerie scene as both of his arms were extended rigidly into the air. I decided to put two extra water purification chlorine tablets into my canteen.

The first day's sweep was a short one and revealed no sign of the enemy. Captain Wong was in constant communication with the boat's commander. By 3 PM it was decided we would wrap up for the day and head back to the boats where we could relax for the remainder of the afternoon. With the early termination of the day's sweep along with Captain Wong's heavy communications, I speculated another mission might be awaiting us.

Back on the boat, the commander, along with Captain Wong, worked out the evening security shift. To minimize the possibility of a sneak attack by the enemy, two and three man crews would be sent ashore at dusk. They would camouflage themselves in the brush and be the first response should a sapper or sniper be on the prowl. The commander also allowed us to get clean by taking a brief swim. He suggested we go in shifts and in groups of no more than four at a time. He cautioned us to stay within arm's length of the boats. We were quick to strip down and take advantage of our new Delta River washing facility. I was glued to my radio and needed to find a replacement to monitor it for me before going in. The commander had encouraged all of us to interact with the South Vietnamese Navy personnel. Given that my counterpart with the red-checkered bandanna was all but stalking me, I figured he was eager to learn. I was just as eager to jump in the river. Wearing nothing more than my shorts, I re-introduced myself. Surprisingly, he did understand a few of my words. Our communication was a mixture of English, French, and Vietnamese with a heavy reliance on sign language. I felt confident he could listen and monitor for a few minutes.

The short swim both cleansed and calmed me. When I returned to the communications center my newfound friend offered to continue monitoring and to listen for any incoming calls. Pointing to his watch, he indicated he would stay until 11 PM, at which time he was scheduled for guard duty. I saw no harm in this. He seemed capable and I felt I was contributing to his learning process. I also felt if there was any truth to rumor number 101, that the U.S. military was going to pull out of Vietnam and would be gradually turning over all responsibilities to the South Vietnamese, he would need all the help and assistance I could give. It was about 8 PM. I told him to wake me if there was any type of transmission on the radio. If there was none, he was to wake me at 11 PM and I would monitor for a few hours before getting relief and turning it over to another. He seemed to understand and assured me several times he would wake me. I finished drying myself from the swim, put on a clean set of shorts and T-shirt and folded my damp towel to make a pillow. For a brief few hours, I had no more thoughts of teaching, no more thoughts of the enemy, no more thoughts of the war, and no more thoughts of these abysmal conditions.

Dazed and disoriented, I awoke from a deep sleep by the frightening and nearby sounds of gunfire. Clearly it had come from the M-60 machine gun that was positioned on the forward deck. I reached for my weapon but, for some reason, did not feel there was a sense of urgency to use it. As I slowly sat up I made a quick scan of the surroundings in an attempt to get a handle on what was happening. There was a moment of complete silence, then suddenly a tremendous amount of commotion including yelling and screaming in Vietnamese. I observed one of the young South Vietnamese officers having a confrontation with the M-60 gunner who apparently had opened fire. I wasn't quite sure what was happening but the officer, who seemed quite infuriated with the gunner, had removed his own helmet and was using it to hit the gunner on the head. There also seemed to be some motion and activity on the riverbank.

Captain Wong and the boat's commander arrived. The commander, attempting to calm things, engaged in conversation with the South Vietnamese officer. I looked at my watch. It was a few minutes past eleven. I wondered why my friend had not awakened me. I got up and walked around to the command center. Monitoring my radio was a different crewmember. I approached Captain Wong.

"What's up?" I asked.

Captain Wong informed me the gunner sitting guard duty had gotten another gunner to relieve him and apparently failed to tell the new person we had an LP out in the brush along the riverbank. The new gunner, not being aware of the LP, spotted some movement in the brush and opened fire, killing one of their own men. I asked if any of our guys were out there. I was told only the Vietnamese Navy was involved and none of our people were out there. Moments later, I watched as some of the crew hurriedly lifted the stretcher that carried the body of the dead soldier on board. A poncho liner was stretched from head to toe.

I went back to my radio to find out who was monitoring it. I introduced myself to the new young RTO and asked him where my friend was. I also pointed to my watch and told him I was supposed to have been called at 11 PM. He looked at my watch and said, "Seiko number one, Seiko number one!"

Again I asked, using sign language along with what little Vietnamese I had learned, "Where was the other RTO?"

The new young replacement RTO stared at me and, after a brief period, shifted his glance down and over to the body on the stretcher. No more questions, I thought. Not taking my eyes off the RTO, I slowly backed away until I was alongside of the stretcher. I gradually knelt down beside the body. I had only lifted the poncho liner a few inches when my eyes came in contact with a portion of the red-checkered bandanna.

RIVERBOAT OPERATION,
THE SECOND 24 HOURS

The next day it was business as usual, with one exception. Captain Wong informed me he would not be going out on the morning's sweep as he had to stay behind to receive a confidential message on a pending B-52 strike. In addition, he would hopefully be giving some advice and guidance to the boat's commander. After last night's incident and with the captain's experience, I am sure there was a lot he could offer. Lieutenant Lesley Hendrickson of Minneapolis, in country since December, would be the acting CO (Command Officer). I would be the lieutenant's command radiotelephone operator. My friend with the red bandanna was bagged, taken ashore, and would be airlifted out. Because of this we had gotten off to a late start. It was around 10 AM. The strength of the morning sun would dutifully set the day's pace.

Never having worked under this new lieutenant, I had to admit I was a little apprehensive. The one thing I did know about him was he always liked to take the point (lead). On this day's sweep, it had been decided the 1st and 2nd platoons would patrol more inland and yet stay parallel to our 3rd and 4th platoons that were patrolling along the riverbanks. This wasn't a correct or acceptable military tactic as there was always the possibility the enemy could work their way in between our two elements and place us at a tactical disadvantage (by shooting at the enemy, you would also be shooting at your own men). In addition, eager to move forward and cover territory, the lieutenant had now taken up the point position. Given the fact the lieutenant was new, I was hesitant to point this out. Also, I did not want to undermine his confidence. Besides, I thought, who the hell knows what they are teaching these guys at Officer's Candidate School? Had I been with Captain Wong, however, I would have for sure quizzed him on these maneuvers. My failure to break silence would later turn out to carry tragic consequences.

It was unusually hot for this time of the morning. I was sweating profusely. We had been on patrol for about an hour with absolutely no sign of the enemy. One thing I noted and had expressed concern to the lieutenant about was the extraordinary amount of traffic being transmitted on my radio. Some of it was in English and some in Vietnamese. I recognized one voice as that of the American Navy commander who appeared to be speaking to one of his South Vietnamese patrol boats or ground forces. I could not figure out why the commander was using my frequency. Could the boat's RTO who was monitoring my radio last night have given him my frequency by accident? Did Captain Wong authorize this, or even know about it? By using my frequency he was effectively tying up and severely limiting any commands and communications that the lieutenant wanted to give to the other platoons. I would speak to Captain Wong about this when I returned.

By 11:30, the lieutenant wanted to know the exact location of the 1st & 2nd platoons. I told him I was not exactly sure, as I had not been able to reach them for the past ten minutes due to the commander's use of our frequency.

"This is bullshit," he said to me. "Give me the horn, I'll clear his ass off my radio."

At the time, we were walking just slightly below an embankment that ran along the river. I was monitoring the radio with the receiver in my left hand. The lieutenant was to my right and slightly behind me. As he grabbed my handset from behind I noticed what appeared to be two empty cans of C-rations on the ground in front of me. I wondered if we had been over this territory before or perhaps even another company had swept this area earlier and left them there. I also noticed a few broken and cut down bamboo shoots just slightly up the embankment and to my right. As observant as I was, what I did not notice was the barrel of an enemy AK-47 protruding from the bushes less than fifteen feet in front of us.

There were two short bursts of fire, perhaps two or three rounds each. The first rounds came within inches of my right ear. My sense of awareness was all the more amplified by the high-pitched resonance of the bullets as they made their way past me. With the second burst of fire I experienced an immediate tightness and choking sensation in my throat. Gasping for breath, I placed my hand to my neck while falling backwards. My first notion was after all these months of heavy combat, without even so much as a scratch, this was the time and place I was going to die. In the back of my mind I knew there was a good possibility of this very thing happening to me sometime. Yet, I couldn't believe the time was now. I thought of an unfinished letter I had written to my friend Jimmy back in Yonkers. I thought of being back at the beach in Truro. I thought of my two sisters, Ann and Laurie.

My next thoughts came as somewhat of a relief. I was not shot. The choking sensation I felt was coming from the heavy radio cord that was attached to my handset and for some reason was now wrapped tightly around my neck. I loosened the cord and immediately grabbed my M-16. While lying flat on my back and looking forward at the bushes where the shots had come, I was anticipating a third round of fire. My will to live was now back in place. Without delay, I raised my weapon. Instinctively, I flipped the safety from off to automatic. Trembling, I took aim at where I suspected the shots came. I pulled back on the trigger to open fire. Silence. Nothing.

I couldn't believe it! My weapon was not firing. Could it be a jam? It's never jammed before. I had a jam at Fort Jackson in basic training but not here. Not in Vietnam. Not in the jungle. Not once. I kept it clean. Why won't it fire? No, wait. Is it possible there is no round in the chamber? Yes, the MPs. The other day. I ejected my round. Holy shit! Dear God…please, please just give me one second to lock in a round. Done.

I sprayed the bushes with my entire ammo clip. I received no return fire. I quickly ejected the empty clip and locked in a new one. Turning to the lieutenant, I called out, "Sir, you okay?" There was no response. Again I called, "Are you…" I never got out the second "okay." I was only a matter of inches from his head. His right hand was clenched tightly to my handset. Since he had fallen backward this would have explained why the wire got wrapped around my neck. His face was totally ashen. His eyes were wide open and staring upwards. He had taken a bullet above the left ear. The blood, completely drained from his head, gave his facial features a totally different and bizarre appearance. For a moment I was in awe of the incredible whiteness of his teeth. He was gone. There was no doubt about this. Echoing from the handset that was within inches from his ear was the familiar voice of the Navy commander.

As my fear was overtaken by anger, I pried the blood-soaked handset from the dead lieutenant's hand and screamed into the mouthpiece.

"Get the fuck off this phone you stupid bastard. Do you read me? Get the fuck off this line and I mean now. Do you read me?" Surprisingly, I had gotten through on the first try as the Navy commander responded, "Are you speaking to me? Please identify, over."

I responded back, "Yes, you asshole, I'm speaking to you. This is the command RTO. We've just been hit, now stay the fuck off this line. The CO is down."

"Will do," came his reply. I immediately contacted the other platoons and warned them of an enemy sniper that may be heading due north along the riverbank. I urged the platoon RTOs to exercise extra caution and reminded them there were friendlies (us) patrolling parallel to each other. I also requested an officer on scene.

Soon after, the 1st platoon's lieutenant arrived and took command. Our medic showed up but could do nothing. We gathered together some bamboo shoots and made a stretcher using the dead lieutenant's poncho liner. On the way back to the boat I had two thoughts on my mind. One, I rarely used foul language. Two, I felt for sure I was heading back to a court-martial for the way I spoke to the Navy commander. Surprisingly, the fact I came within inches of taking a bullet in the head did not even cross my mind. War can easily play tricks with you. In very subtle ways, it can even rearrange your priorities.

Once back on the boat, Captain Wong inquired how I was doing. Without looking him in the face and staring out at the river I responded, "Okay." I remember thinking, had he pursued his line of questioning as to my state of mind I would, in all probability, have broken down. Continuing with business, he requested a complete debriefing of the events that led up to our being ambushed. Attending were the officers from the other platoons, along with all the other RTOs.

In anticipation of a confrontation with the Navy commander, I removed my radio and placed it in a secure location off to the side. I remained standing. Maybe a court-martial would get me out of this hellhole, I thought. Inside, by the communications center, I observed the commander as he was speaking with one of the South Vietnamese officers. The commander stood about six foot six and could easily pass for a John Wayne look-a-like. Finishing business with the officer, he abruptly turned and stared my way. Slowly he approached me. Intuitively, I felt he knew I was the one mouthing off to him on the radio. He came to within a few inches of where I was standing. He glanced briefly at my blood-soaked fatigues. He then looked me directly in the eye. Raising both hands and placing them on my shoulders he asked, "You okay, son?"

"Yes, sir," I replied, failing to look him in the eye. There was a long pause and then he added, "You did real fine out there."

He had caught me off guard. At best, I was anticipating a reprimand; at worst, charges brought against me for disrespecting an officer. What I had not expected was this attitude of sympathy and support, tolerance and understanding. This was not what I was prepared for. However, after what I had just gone through, it was exactly what I needed. Suddenly, the six-foot-six-inch frame of the Navy commander hovering over me just became, in my eyes, that much bigger. After his humbling concern, I broke the moment's silence.

"I apologize for my comments on the air, sir,"

"No apologies necessary, son, you did what was necessary. You did fine."

Lieutenant Hendrickson was placed on deck and lay covered up in the center of our group. Captain Wong informed me there was no need to call in for a dust-off (helicopter) as he had already made the request and one was en route. By the way he spoke to me, I could sense the pain he felt losing one of his men. Perhaps he felt a little guilty for not being able to be out there with us this morning. Maybe he even felt it could have, or should have been he and not the lieutenant. The captain was particularly quiet and somber. The medic, along with a few of the men, began placing the lieutenant in a body bag. By mid-afternoon the lieutenant was airlifted out. Searching for solace I sought out and found a section of the boat where I could lie down. I needed to be by myself. I did my best to get some rest.

At 4 PM, I was awakened by sounds of activity, commotion and yelling. It all seemed to be coming from the patrol boat docked next to us. John Paxson came up and kneeled down beside me.

"How you doing?" he asked. I liked John very much. There were times he was a bit too serious. Then there were times his desert-dry and macabre sense of humor did reality checks with us. He had been living in Freeport, Grand Bahamas and moved to Michigan prior to the war, and when I first arrived at the base camp, John was the very first person that took the time to introduce himself to me and show me around.

"I'm okay," I responded. "What's with all the excitement next door?"

"Oh, not a whole lot," he said rather nonchalantly. "Just that they captured the sniper that almost blew your "f'n" head off, that's all."

"Are you serious?" I said in a state of disbelief.

He just gave me one of his shit-ass grins as he nodded his head up and down. "Had a feeling you'd be interested. I was just over there. Come on, let's go."

It wasn't every day you had an opportunity to come face-to-face with the one shooting at you. In fact it was quite unusual. Generally the enemy was heavily camouflaged and hiding behind the brush. After an attack, if he weren't killed, he would run. For me, meeting this person could only be therapeutic. As we made our way over to the neighboring boat I was glad to have John by my side. I truly didn't know how I was going to respond to the sight of the sniper. I did know at the time, John was stable enough to keep me in check should my emotions get the better of me.

As we boarded the back of the boat I saw several men from the 1st and 2nd platoons who had not gone out on this morning's patrol and had wandered over to get a glimpse of the enemy sniper. With all the people and all the turmoil there appeared to be almost a carnival-like atmosphere. What was happening, I thought? Then one of the guys from the 1st platoon spotted me and yelled out, "Hey man, the fuck'n gook that almost "offed" you is up front."

John, his dry wit in full gear, and quick to defuse situations that might become volatile, commented, "Amazing... he is capable of putting together an entire sentence."

I decided not to go forward where I would be face-to-face with the sniper. Instead I chose to climb to the upper deck, where I could take a look from a distance. John stayed with me as I made my way forward and up to the small deck of the bridge that overlooked the bow of the boat.

"Well, there he is," John said.

For a moment, all I could see were a few of our guys along with a crowd of the South Vietnamese Navy people. They had a prisoner and it seemed they were making the most of it. As yet, I couldn't see the captive. I could hear the men shouting obscenities and making fun of their new prize. I had to keep in mind this was not the American Navy here, and, for the most part, the South Vietnamese were the ones yelling the insults and calling the shots. Suddenly, a Vietnamese officer shouted out something from the distance. Just as suddenly, the group began to slowly back away, allowing me, for the first time, to take a good look at my newfound adversary. Truly, I wasn't prepared for the sight in front of me.

He was standing in an upright position. His hands had been tied behind his back. A rope had been wrapped around his ankles and chest and attached to the flagpole that stood behind him. A blindfold was wrapped around his eyes. His upper left arm was poorly wrapped with a blood-soaked bandage. He was completely nude. He was also a boy. At best he couldn't have been more than 15 years of age and very possibly younger.

This boy that now stood before me both carefully and callously killed one of our people. I have no doubt whatsoever that had fate allowed, he would surely have done the same to me. Yet, at that very moment, he had my complete and unconditional sympathy.

Off in the distance, the faint sound of a helicopter could be heard.

"What will happen to him?" I asked John.

"They are flying in an intelligence officer who will take him back to TOC for questioning. That's probably the chopper now," he responded.

"Then what happens?" I asked. Exercising his dry wit, "In all probability, they'll give him some ice cream and teach him the error of his ways. Then they'll give him some money and invite him to join our side."

As the helicopter neared, Ken Luedke, one of the other RTOs, approached the boy. Luedke (we called him Lucky) was a tall lanky kid from Long Island. I guessed him to be about 19 years of age. He was a good and conscientious RTO. He was also what we called "good people." I liked him and had hoped he would take over my position when I got off line. Disregarding the officer's command to keep back, Lucky came to within a few inches of the boy's face and began to shout obscenities. At this moment, the feelings he harbored for this young sniper were anything but attuned to mine.

Leaving John, I made my way down from the bridge and walked towards Lucky. I respected Lucky and could easily identify with his anger. On any given mission, we RTOs are second in line to the enemy's primary target. But this wasn't the time or place to vent our frustrations. I asked Lucky to cool it.

"Mac, what do you mean? This kid almost blew your fuck'n head off," he responded in absolute bewilderment.

"He's just a kid, Lucky, just a kid. Let's cut him some slack," I replied. The boy was trembling and in all probability feared for his life.

Lying about on the deck were a half dozen or so military belts that belonged to the Navy crew members. Attached to the belts were ammo pouches, canteens, holsters and first aid packs. Grabbing one of them I removed two large ace bandages. Tying them together and creating a swath I approached the naked boy. Very gently, I wrapped it around his waist. "No sweat," I whispered to him. "No sweat." After a brief period, his trembling subsided. Within a month he'll be on our side working for us, I thought, as I backed away. Moments later the sounds, shouts and commotion of the military intelligence officers could be heard as they made their way forward.

"Is there any ice cream on board this tin can?" one of them yelled out.

THE MISSION

March 1969

Dearest David,

Last night your father called Judge Couzens a busybody at the Yonkers City Club after the Judge said (his wife) Mary Jane had gotten two letters from you. The Judge then took a swing at your father knocking him to the ground. No charges were filed but believe they both dined earlier with "Johnny Walker."

Love,

The Mother

PS – Walk on the sidewalk

I believe I was well trained by the United States Army. They taught me the art of jungle warfare and survival skills. However, they left out how to react when you lose someone you care about. Just a few weeks earlier, while on a break during a search and destroy mission, four North Vietnamese soldiers casually strolled into our area. Our offensive positions were only partially set up. Pete Arnone, the 3rd platoon's M-60 machine gunner, with weapon in place and ready to go, had just finished eating and was in the process of taking a puff on a small cigar. He was also the first to come face-to-face with these NVAs. Pete immediately jumped on his weapon and let go a short burst of fire. The four soldiers went down. Suddenly without any warning we were engulfed in enemy fire. It was coming from all directions. And it was heavy. Not just bullets, but also RPGs (rocket propelled grenades). It was obvious the four Pete hit were only the point men of a much larger enemy force, perhaps even the size of a company. Pete, with every intention of making sure his next burst of fire would be considerably longer than the last, applied pressure to the trigger of his M-60 only to find his weapon had jammed. For him, it really wouldn't have made a difference whether his weapon fired or not as, seconds later, an exploding RPG round saturated his body with bits and pieces of hot metal. Pete was hit badly.

There were many other casualties but it was the loss of Peter that affected me the most. He was the first of our group to have been wounded. The others, John Paxson, Roger Wasson and Miles 'Doc' Touchberry would soon face similar fates. Pete had taken his job as an M-60 machine gun operator very seriously. He was methodical and meticulous about keeping his weapon clean. Its jamming was a fluke. It was also a first. I had mixed feelings about Pete's being hit. The compassionate side of me was concerned for his well-being. Yet a darker side of me had my thoughts centered on who would now protect me the next time we engaged the enemy. Now, on this mission, I was minus the security and companionship of my New York friend, Pete Arnone.

Today's mission, like so many others, had started with little notice. With less than twelve hours notification, our company was given orders to be airlifted from our base camp and flown into what army intelligence suspected to be an enemy Viet Cong campground. Over the past few weeks our contact with the enemy was on an almost daily basis. They were basically referred to as minor skirmishes: a firefight here, a sniper there. Yet our casualty count was unusually high.

Our injured came from enemy fire, from friendly fire (our own) and even from accidents. (When you have a situation when fewer than twenty-four months ago, over fifty percent of the now existing battlefield manpower were sitting in a classroom, halfway attentive to the lecture of the week, or running field goals for their local high schools, accidents are bound to happen.) It was not a good period of time for any of us. Morale was low, and the men were exceptionally edgy.

Company B, our company, was made up of four platoons and at full strength consisted of between eighty to one-hundred men. We were down a good number on this particular mission. As the captain's radiotelephone operator, figuratively and certainly unofficially, I had the ambiguous distinction of being second in charge. Or so it seemed. He gave the commands. I saw they were communicated to all the other RTOs. I received very few complaints barking the captain's orders. It was a demanding position, yet it had its perks. (Because of the weight of my radio, I didn't have to carry extra supplies or ammunition, and officers, for the most part, treated me respectfully.) Of course, the one real downside was, on all missions, the captain was a prime target for enemy snipers. This alone could ruin your entire day. Carrying his radio, you had to be within arm's reach at all times. More often than not, when a call came in for the captain you would hand him the handset, then turn your back to him to scout the surrounding area for suspected enemy movement.

The airlift for this mission came in two shifts, the first of which consisted of fifteen helicopters. Our command group was on the first flight. The takeoff and landing went smoothly. We encountered no hostile fire, nor did we detect any enemy movement. We were set down in a large open field. Several miles off to our south was a wood line that appeared to be endless. Knowing that was our objective, its mere presence appeared to be somewhat ominous. Captain Wong sent out two teams of men to set up observation posts. The orders were given to spread out, secure the area and wait for the remainder of our men to arrive.

It was approximately 2:00 PM. By 3:30, the unmistakable and always welcoming sounds of hueys (helicopters) could be heard off in the distance. I radioed the head pilot and informed him the landing zone was secure and there were friendlies (U.S. troops) on the ground. I repeated and emphasized the word friendlies. Assigned to each of the hueys were two door gunners. They sat behind M-60 machine guns. It was their job to saturate the area with as much firepower as possible just prior to landing. Their role was a crucial and dangerous one that very often was played out several times a day. The only treasure greater to the enemy than a captured G.I. was the shooting down of a helicopter. Door gunners were an attractive and prized target.

At 500 feet in the air and several miles off, it is easy to mistake a U.S. force for that of the enemy. I felt a need to relay to the pilots my "friendlies-on-the-ground" communiqué for a third time. The lead pilot assured me all door gunners were aware and he thanked me for my thoroughness. Within minutes, the wind-swept dust from the landing of the hueys encompassed our troops. The remaining part of

53

our company landed without incident. I radioed the Tactical Operations Center and notified them the landing went well and all troops were on the ground.

Captain Wong headed over to meet with the leader of the second platoon to review the operation and strategy. His name was Jerrie Ramage. Soon after, under the heat of the late afternoon sun, the men of Bravo Company along with their deadly equipment began to head south, single file, towards the wood line and the suspected enemy camp grounds. It was just after 4 PM. We had a little over three hours of remaining daylight.

Within that period of time we had to reach our destination, secure a campsite, prepare for our offensive by setting up machine gun positions and anti-personnel (claymore) mines. We would then lie in wait to ambush the hopefully unsuspecting enemy. That was our schedule. That was our itinerary. Of course, the enemy had theirs.

Time was of the essence. I felt we had gotten off to a late start. One of the guys started repeating an old rhyme: "It's late, it's late, and Charlie moves at eight." It was unsettling. I had every confidence our forces controlled the daylight hours. I also knew the evening belonged to Charlie. That was a given. The overwhelming majority of our missions and their successes depended heavily upon the fact we were to be set up, dug in and secure prior to the sun falling. Rarely would a company of our size move at night.

It was a little after six o'clock when the entire element came to a complete standstill. We were still a good distance from the edge of the forest. Anticipating the question from Captain Wong, I radioed ahead to the RTO of the first platoon.

"Romeo Tango One, Romeo Tango One, this is Charlie Papa - - what's up? Why have we stopped? Over."

"Charlie Papa, this is Romeo Tango One. Be advised, our point man came across a small campsite. Over," was his response.

Several weeks back I had received a similar call from one of the RTOs. At that time I had asked how large was the site? The question and answer took no more than five seconds. Immediately after, we received enemy gunfire. Instinctively, in situations such as this I knew it was better to ask questions in the prone position rather than standing up. Without asking permission, I radioed all units.

"Hit the dirt, get down, hit the dirt, we've got activity."

At the time, one of the many differences between our forces and the enemy was, in certain areas, discipline. They had it and, for the most part, we lacked it. Perhaps this was due in part to knowing and believing in what you were fighting for. Truly, the enemy was several steps ahead of us and a lot more clear on this than we were. We just did not want to be where we were. However, when an order is given for our troops to "hit the dirt," it is done with the speed, timing and precision of a Swiss timepiece. Without exception, no one was standing.

Captain Wong immediately asked, "What have we got?"

"Campsite, sir," I said and continued transmitting. "Romeo Tango One, this is Charlie Papa, any movement or activity? Over."

"Negative on movement, but activity is recent. Over." I relayed this to the captain. Although Captain Wong had, I believe, absolute faith in my accuracy, he was also a hands-on officer. Wanting to hear first hand from the lieutenant on site, he grabbed my handset.

"Romeo Tango One, this is Papa, this is Papa. How recent, how many? Over."

"Papa, this is Romeo Tango One, I'd say three, maybe four. The campfire is still warm. Must have heard us coming and 'dideyed' (ran) out of here. Over."

At that point, Captain Wong ordered all platoons to fan out and move parallel to the wood line. Our movements were slow. The heat and humidity were taking a toll on the men. Twice within a short period of time we stopped for a water break. We exercised caution as we approached the wooded area which was no more than a few hundred feet away. There was some discussion between Captain Wong and Sgt. Ramage as to whether a "recon by fire" was called for at this time. ("Recon by fire" was a reconnaissance of an area without moving an inch. If an area was highly suspect and had the potential of harboring the enemy, the men would be ordered to open fire with whatever weapon they had. Its purpose was threefold. First, by firing into a suspected enemy area, you were trying to draw their fire, thereby exposing and pinpointing their positions. Second, it allowed all the new people to get a little experience testing their weapons in the field, while getting a taste of what an actual firefight, one-sided as it may be, might be like. Third, strange as it may sound, it was also a pacifier. It took the edge off many of the guys. By firing their weapons, the men were able to let off a little steam.)

There was a downside to this and its factor had to be weighed heavily. By engaging in a 'recon by fire' with the massive amount of fire power we carried, you were in effect giving your position away. You would be sacrificing a future and potential element of surprise. And in jungle warfare, losing the element of surprise can carry a high price tag. Because of the lateness in the day, Sgt. Ramage was not in favor of this. Captain Wong agreed and with that it was decided to forego the "recon by fire."

We kept moving. Soon after, Captain Wong and I came across the small campsite that was radioed into us earlier. The command was given to halt the troops and for the men to take the prone position while we studied the abandoned site. We were on high alert. We expected contact with the enemy at any time. Captain Wong kneeled down and placed his hands slightly above the ashes. Warm. Half a dozen empty cans of C-rations were left behind.

"Well, I guess these guys won't be giving us any trouble," I said.

"What do you mean?" asked the captain.

"The C-rations… they're American, sir," I responded.

"So?" the captain said.

"Sir," I continued, "they've got to be suffering from food poisoning!"

"Very funny, Mac," the captain responded. "Is that why you gave me your beans and franks last week?"

Humor played an important role in war. It would help to keep you in focus and remind you there is life beyond all this. Whenever a situation for amusement presented itself, I took full advantage of it. Captain Wong was one of my prime targets.

We were halfway into a lighthearted laugh when we spotted the helmet. It was in an upright position and off to the side of the smoldering campfire. A band around the base was lined with long pieces of grass and weeds for camouflage. The helmet was partially hidden by vegetation, making it difficult to have been seen by the point man and the first platoon. It did not appear to be booby-trapped. Instinctively, I sensed what Captain Wong was thinking.

"NVA?" I asked.

The captain didn't respond. Instead he leaned over to pick it up.

"Be careful, sir, it could be a booby trap!" I yelled.

Silence.

"Is that what I think it is, sir?" I continued.

Again, silence. Captain Wong, a gentleman of very few words, was a fine officer and one of the best I served under. Military code and protocol teaches in all cases, "the mission (not the men) come first." Captain Wong walked a very fine line with this code. The mission was always of the utmost importance to him and he had always carried it out to the best of his ability. His accomplishments for attaining a high enemy body count were considerable and well-known throughout the 25th Infantry Division. He also showed an intense and profound concern for the health, well-being and safety of his men. He took care of them.

At the end of a firefight, when you had to account for who was hit and on what side, he would seem somewhat pleased to learn we had killed one or more of the enemy. However, if one of his men was wounded or killed, he displayed a sense of anger at the enemy, and at times took it personally. The intimate gaze of his deep dark eyes could rarely conceal the anguish he fostered when he lost one of his men.

His silence finally broken, speaking softly, almost in a whisper, "So, we've got NVA out here. Radio all platoons to move out and proceed with caution. Inform them of possible NVA in the area. Notify TOC headquarters what we've found. And Mac, keep both ears to the handset."

If Captain Wong seemed concerned, he had good reason to be. The mission we were on was to search out and destroy a suspected Vietcong enemy campground. We were well equipped and prepared. But hard hats, or military helmets such as the one Captain Wong had just come across were not a part of Charlie's wardrobe which consisted basically of black pajamas and a straw hat. A helmet such as this belonged to the more infamous North Vietnamese Army. This was a different ball game entirely.

"Charlie" slept during the day and played at night. Booby-traps, sniper and small arms fire were more his method. Harassment of the troops was his code. Hit, maim and run was his game. For sure, there were many times when the Vietcong organized themselves into groups and even small companies and stoutly attacked our base camps. But it was not commonplace for them to get beyond or into our well-fortified perimeters. Their weapons were little match for the lethal and overwhelming arsenal that lay within our realm.

The North Vietnamese were well trained, well organized and far better equipped than the Vietcong. They were exceptionally disciplined and highly motivated. They were clear on their cause to fight and greatly determined to win. They would boldly attack in daylight hours and fight to the death. This was their land. To them, we were the enemy. Coming across the helmet was not a good sign, and though not prone to premonitions, I did not have a good feeling about this mission, nor about the evening to come.

Arriving at the base of the wood line, I admired the beauty and splendor of the towering trees. But they seemed to amplify the early stages of the rapidly growing evening darkness. (It's late, it's late... and Charlie moves at eight, I mused.)

The coolness of my sweat from the many hours of marching suddenly turned to a chill. Silently, the men began to strip off their gear. Daylight was ending and body language danced with communication. A nod of the head here, a lift of the hand there. Slowly, positions were taken. Cautiously, the various offensive armaments were laid in place. The lethal decorations set up, our deadly welcome mat was out. The stage was now set for what was to be our shelter, our habitat and our ambush site for the next twelve hours.

One of the few perks of being command RTO was you didn't necessarily have to perform guard duty and, if things were going smoothly and your mind was set to it, you could even get a little extra sleep. This evening I felt uneasy and restless. Voluntarily, I offered to take first watch. Smitty, one of the new guys in our company, was assigned second watch. He would start at 10 PM and go until midnight, if he didn't fall asleep, which happens, or get himself shot, which happens. There would be four other two-hour shifts after him, taking us to whatever safety and security the daylight had to offer.

These were the hours when silence was golden and movement, for the sake of preservation, was kept to an all time minimum. Even those poor souls with over-active bladders did their best to "go" before we bedded down, or do it in their pants at a later hour. A lack of discipline in this area could easily make you a target to the enemy. A stream of urine falling onto six month old dried leaves and vegetation had a way of echoing throughout the woods, and if the stars or moon caught you at the right angle, you might just as well be displaying a flashlight with a revolving beacon on top.

With a final review of our location and grid, Captain Wong finished up what was supposed to have been his last communiqué with TOC headquarters for the night. As he prepared for the evening, the jungle colored poncho liner he carried would offer him comfort but the firmness of the ground would deprive him of sleep.

"You okay, Mac?" he whispered to me. I liked it when he called me "Mac." That was my nickname in high school and it would always conjure up pleasant memories.

"I would be better off if I were in Hawaii!" I said, poking a little fun at his home state.

The light of the stars had thrown a gentle glow on his silhouette and, although my joke was met by silence, I was comforted by the broad grin that beamed across his face.

Boredom, loneliness, fear, and sometimes religion can often be the key ingredients for sitting guard duty. Of course, the fact you are responsible for the early warning of any approaching enemy carries its weight. This particular evening was a clear one. The air was warm, the winds were gentle, and the endless display of stars had graced the fields out front with a soft light. With the peacefulness of the setting, artificial though it may have been, my mind wandered, thinking five years back to the age of seventeen.

At the time, with my parents' marital problems at their peak, I had the freedom to escape Westchester on the weekends and visit New York City. Sometimes I would invite my close friend, Steve, from New Rochelle, or Jimmy from Yonkers, to come along with me. Many times we attended Broadway shows.

On this particular evening, as I sat guard duty, I was thinking of the many similarities to that of attending a Broadway show. Depending upon your location, and your frame of mind, you could be sitting orchestra, mezzanine or balcony. The only real difference was you never knew whether comedy or drama would be taking center stage.

This evening, although mentally I had started out in orchestra, I found myself drifting back to upper balcony. My mind was anywhere but where it should have been on this warm and breezy night. I remember becoming relaxed and at peace with myself. Checking the time, I realized my watch had well over-lapped into Smitty's. I remember thinking he should appreciate having to do less than the scheduled two-hour guard duty. As with anyone I also wanted to caution him about not falling asleep. My watch was uneventful and, hopefully, his would be also. As I stood up and leaned over the captain's body, the evening silence was broken by a radio transmission.

Quickly I returned to my sitting position. Like so many other nights, I anticipated the call to be from one of our platoons that was alerting us to enemy movement out front. Instead, the call was from TOC headquarters. The time: 11:30 PM. They wanted to speak to the captain.

Not wanting to wake him up at this hour for some frivolous message that could wait until morning, I responded:

"This is Charlie Papa (command post), this is Charlie Papa. What's up? Papa (the captain) is resting. Anything I need to pass on? Over."

TOC came back with, "That's a negative Charlie Papa. Get him on the horn and I mean now, son!"

At this point Captain Wong was in the process of sitting up and looking around. As he reached out for the telephone handset he inquired, "What have we got, Mac?"

A call at this hour, whether from TOC headquarters or closer by, from one of our platoons, had to be of a serious nature. Hearing only one side of the conversation, I listened as attentively as possible while at the same time, cautiously keeping a sharp lookout beyond the wood line and into the wide open fields. For sure, I was now seated center row orchestra.

MIRACLE ON 34th GRID

Coming from a somewhat dysfunctional family (my father being a Roman Catholic, my mother, a Protestant, with constant in-house fighting in front of the children that finally ended in divorce), I had been placed in the unique situation of experiencing two religions for the price of one.

From a financial standpoint, my father did take care of the family, though he was rarely home. The one day you could count on his being home was Sunday. For many years, in the early morning hours, I attended services with my mother at Saint Paul's Protestant Church on Palisade Avenue. Afterwards, it was off with my father to the Sacred Heart Roman Catholic Church on Shonnard Terrace, or Christ the King Church on Broadway.

During a firefight in the jungles of Vietnam, religion and personal beliefs have a curious way of cropping up, occupying, fulfilling and even sometimes validating certain convictions. I couldn't even begin to tell you the number of times I witnessed young men faced with certain death cry out. Sometimes it was for their mother. Sometimes it was for their father. Most often the cries I heard were "Oh God," "Dear God," "God help me," "Jesus Christ," and "Mary Mother of God." The cries I heard would sometimes be frightening. They could be heard at the peak of battle in the middle of night when all hell had broken loose. Or during quieter times, midway through the day, after a sniper's bullet had completed its mission. These cries echoed with a sense of finality. The dangers found in this distant land so far away from home were fully eminent and certainly always constant, for this reason the cliché that there truly are no atheists in foxholes.

On this particular mission, with more than eight hours remaining before the arrival of daylight, I would be a witness to and marvel at that most extraordinary of all events, the phenomenon of a miracle.

Captain Wong continued his transmissions with TOC headquarters. Though I hadn't the slightest idea what was going on, I didn't like it one bit. What I did know was our location was in the general area of the grid squares on the map he had been referring to. We were at the far northeast end of grid G26, with the open field being grids 27, 28, 29 and so on.

After a number of transmissions, Captain Wong handed me the handset and ordered me to get all the platoon leaders on the line. At best this would only take a few moments. As I concluded my transmission to the RTO of the first platoon, requesting he get his platoon leader on the phone, Captain Wong grabbed the handset away from me and started calling the others on his own. There was tenseness in his voice. Clearly he was agitated. All I could do was sit and watch, listen and wait. The conversations between the captain, the platoon leaders and TOC headquarters intensified. I picked up bits and pieces here and there. Gradually, it became clear to me what was going down. I was absolutely dumbfounded.

Preparations had been made from "higher up" for a predawn air strike. A breakdown in communications between TOC and the "higher-ups" had left Captain Wong unaware. It was scheduled to happen sometime between 4 and 5 AM. The designated target was only a few miles from our location. There were good reasons for Captain Wong to be concerned. It wasn't just any air strike. They were multiple groups of the deadly B-52 bombers. The planes, dispatched from Clark Air Force Base in the Philippines, were already air-born and not likely to be called back. Our campsite was within fallout range. Unless we moved, and moved soon, there was little doubt we would be in harm's way. Understandably, getting orders to move in the dead of night, in unfamiliar territory with recent signs and evidence of enemy activity, was very risky.

Captain Wong had to be troubled. Moving an element of our size in the dark with a combination of experienced and inexperienced men had the potential to draw friendly-fire. All it takes is for one guy to get "spooked" and anyone can be shooting at anyone. The old cliché "itchy trigger finger" was a truth and taken very seriously by the seasoned veterans on line. There were two types to watch closely that were a potential high risk to a friendly-fire-incident.

Type A: the very young or new recruit who had no or few experiences with engaging the enemy.

Type B: a select few of the "old-timers" – ones who had been on line for a long time and had unwittingly slipped over the edge with one too many battles.

The time was half past twelve. The odds for a peaceful night were rapidly diminishing for Captain Wong.

Stepping out from the shadows of the forest the men of Bravo Company, 1st Battalion, 27th Infantry Brigade began to fall into formation. Some were half asleep. Most hadn't the slightest idea what was happening or why we were now on the move. Whispers of questions and rumors permeated up and down the line. We marched in single formation. We stretched out over a distance of a quarter mile. Captain Wong did not say much to me during the first half-hour, but I knew my communication responsibilities: keep the men in line, keep eyes focused on the man in front, don't shoot the man in front.

I relayed this information to all of the platoon RTOs emphasizing the latter. I also asked permission of Captain Wong if I could request the safety on all weapons be turned on which would hopefully avoid any potential accidental firing. He agreed. We were obviously on the same page regarding the threat of a friendly-fire incident as he ordered me to make sure the M-79s, (grenade launchers) which some of the men carried were loaded but not locked (cocked) for purposes of safety. The M-79 was capable of discharging a number of various offensive and defensive rounds of ammunition from a shotgun blast to the launching of a grenade, from popping smoke to firing tear gas. To be sure, the M-79 was a unique and versatile weapon. It was also unpredictably delicate and, unless properly handled, had a tendency to sometimes discharge accidentally.

Not wanting to be left completely in the dark I expressed my concern about where we were going. The captain explained we were simply following the trail we used yesterday leading us away from our campsite. He also added TOC had arranged for two CRIP (Combined Reconnaissance and Intelligence Platoon) members, who were highly knowledgeable of the terrain, to meet us somewhere around the 29th grid. The CRIP members, or scouts as they were sometimes called, would work under Captain Wong to guide us out of and away from the B-52 projected fallout zone. That's just great, I thought! Let's see, we're walking in the middle of a known enemy territory. There's a chance I might be shot by one of our own men. A B-52 strike is about to happen soon, with a likelihood of hot bits and pieces of flying scrap metal landing on me, and oh, yes, one other thing: two complete strangers, probably armed to the hilt, are about to jump out in front of us at any time without warning. I couldn't help but think about what the current temperature might be in Toronto.

The time was half past one. We had been on the march for about an hour now in very close formation when suddenly I smacked right up against McCabe, the guy in front of me. In turn, Captain Wong bumped into me. At that very moment, with handset held to my ear, I heard the RTO from the 2nd platoon in front of us call in. "Hold up, hold up, we've just come across two scouts. Tell Papa (the captain) we're sending them down the line to you. Better inform the 1st to hold up or they'll continue marching to Hanoi."

The captain gave me the order to hold up and "take five." While we waited for the CRIP members to arrive, the RTO from the 2nd platoon got on the line and whispered to no one in particular, "You know we almost blew their stupid-ass heads off, popping out of the bushes without any warning and no calling card or noth'n. This is bullshit, man. Someone's gonna get hurt." Another RTO somberly joked, "I'd of offed them."

When it came to transmitting, for the most part the RTOs displayed proper etiquette in getting their messages across. Unless a mission had ended or orders given to head back for a 24-hour stand-down, it was unusual for any of them to break discipline. I had no doubt these scouts came within inches of losing their lives. I would like to think my constant warnings of caution to the men to watch out for friendly-fire avoided a near calamity. Whatever, the men were edgy.

"Good evening, gents," said one of the scouts who wore a camouflaged bush hat and spoke with a heavy English accent. "I understand that you're in sort of a pickle and the Air Force made you run off and all that. Well, not to worry, we know this ground. Got good "intel." Also, got good light and visibility from the stars, so no problem there. No NVA in my direction so we shan't associate with them. But Chuck *is* out there, so we must be hushed and all. If you gents have no questions we do need to press on." Captain Wong had no questions, but I was wondering why the Englishman referred to Charlie as Chuck? Did he have some sort of formal run-in at one time with him? He acted so proper, I thought.

After a brief period of time we were on the march again. I figured at the pace we were traveling we had at least another two to three hours to go to get safely away from the target area. I felt a bit of relief having the scouts out front leading us through territory they were familiar with. Also, they did make a point that with the stars being out we would have good visibility.

By 2:30 AM my entire body was overcome with exhaustion. I had been up and without rest for nearly twenty-four hours. I was tired. I felt weak. Using the coverage of darkness, I considered getting rid of some of the supplies I had been carrying. I began to make some mental notes and review what I might be able to get rid of and still be capable of carrying out my duties as RTO. I think I packed six cans of C-rations, which were to take care of breakfast, lunch and dinner. Or was it seven cans? I could skip lunch and have only a snack for dinner. That's four, maybe even five I could get rid of. That would lighten the weight a bit. I also had three spare batteries for the radio. They were heavy. I was only required to carry one spare. But I didn't know the length of the mission so I carried a second for an emergency backup. The third I carried as an extra for the other RTOs. Then, for whatever reason, I began to think about my mother. What if Mom found out about what I was about to do, I amusedly thought. Oh, shit. Where the hell is that sidewalk she wants me to walk on? And what I wouldn't give to just lie down for five minutes. But I had no choice. As did all the others, I continued to march.

It was now close to 3 AM. I remember staring ahead and, for just a moment or two, losing sight of McCabe who was no more than a few feet in front of me. Am I passing out? I wondered. The mind can play tricks on you without sleep. I thought back to my days of basic training at Ft. Jackson and being awake for twenty-two hours during an all night ambush exercise. There, around 4 AM, I thought for sure I saw this big pink elephant walking in and out of the woods. I never told anyone that story. No, wait, there's McCabe. I can see him now. I'm okay. Tired, but okay. Hang on a second, he's gone again. What the hell? What's this all about? What's happening? I have to tell Captain Wong.

As I turned to alert Captain Wong I was startled to observe I could scarcely recognize his stout silhouette as he walked behind me. Without saying anything I glanced upwards to the sky. My exhaustion turned to alarm when I saw well over half the stars were now covered by an enormous bank of thick clouds. What little light we had remaining from the few stars I could see would soon be covered for sure by a second bank that was rapidly moving in. Sensing my concern and knowing the very valid danger of moving in absolute and total darkness the captain spoke, "Mac, we've got to keep on the move. Stay in touch with all units. Hands on shoulders if necessary. No one fires without my orders. Understand? No one! We can do this."

A new sense of responsibility, inspired by Captain Wong, gave me my second wind. I was as alert now as having just come out of an eight-hour sleep, though my fear of friendly-fire was still very real. I needed to be prepared for a worst case scenario, I thought. After all, we were nearly in total darkness. Having made a resolution I would not be first to open fire, I aimed my weapon down and pointed it towards the ground. I double-checked my safety to make sure it was in the on position. If one of our guys was going to shoot at me, I was comfortable and capable in my determination not to shoot back. For whatever reason, our pace had picked up considerably, which only added to our overall dilemma. Once again McCabe disappeared in front. I wasn't even a hundred percent sure I was walking on the same path as him. I attempted to call the other platoons to pass along the captain's message. I also wanted to find out how they were coping. Hopefully they would not detect my sense of trepidation.

Instead, all I could do was listen in on a steady flow of incoming transmissions. One RTO after another: "Man, it's dark out here."

"Where the hell is Johnson? I can't see Johnson."

"We got to stop."

"I almost tripped over Sergeant Rodrigues. How the heck do they expect us to see where we're go'n?"

Listening to all the transmissions, I came to recognize the various roles that were now being played out by each and every one of the RTOs. Up until this evening, it had been I and I alone who had articulated the captain's commands. Now I fully understood and accepted a new role as the captain's RTO. They needed to vent, and this was one situation I was not ready, willing or wanting to defuse. I let them have their say.

Soon after, there was a pause in all the chatter, then a new transmission from the lieutenant of the first platoon: "Break, break, break. This is Papa Lima one. This is crap. We're in p-soup, I can't see my men, let me speak to Papa." Keeping my pace, I turned to Captain Wong to hand him my handset. Seeing nothing I reached out and felt the barrel of an M-16. Hope this is his, I thought. In the darkness, someone placed a hand on mine. As I passed the handset over, I was relieved to hear the captain's voice.

The captain and the lieutenant discussed options. No one could see anyone with the above cloud cover. For obvious reasons, flashlights were not a part of night ambush attire. The officers carried penlights for map reading, but this was scarcely the thing to use to light the way and provide the necessary guidance. After communicating with all the platoon leaders, Captain Wong was faced with having to make a decision. Clearly, he had only two choices. Equally, he would shoulder heavy potential consequences.

The first choice was to stop the company completely. The costs here were threefold.

He would be disobeying an order from TOC headquarters. His company would be exposed in the open, without the safeguard of cover and in the center of a path that was well traveled by the enemy. If one of the B-52 bombers were as much as a few seconds off from the designated release and drop zones, our company could well be the center point of ground zero.

The second choice would be to continue the march. The consequences here were the very real possibility of friendly-fire among the men, not to mention the likelihood of losing some of the men by getting separated and lost in the dark. Captain Wong, deciding the latter was the lesser of two evils, opted to continue the march.

It was a little after 3 AM as I considered the odds of someone soon getting hurt. In my mind I reviewed the new procedures for the calling of a medevac, a call I made countless times in the past. More recently, however, the operator taking my calls would decline to dispatch a medevac unless and until I gave a detailed description of the wounds along with an accurate count of the injured or killed. The medevacs would have to use landing lights, I thought. I have to think about that. I would also have to give our location. Our location? I didn't even know our location. I turned to Captain Wong and asked him if he knew our position. "Well, I can only give you an approximate," he said. "But my guess is that from the bend I could see in the wood line that we passed before we lost light... I'd say we just entered the 34th grid."

Grid 34, I thought. We hadn't altered direction so I assumed we were still in G section. Moments passed.

"Tango Oscar Charlie (TOC headquarters), Tango Oscar Charlie, this Charlie Papa, we've got three wounded from friendly-fire. They are all M-16 rifle wounds. One is a chest wound with severe bleeding. The others are leg and arm. I am requesting a dust-off at grid G34," I mimicked into the handset without pressing the transmit button. Come on, Dave, I thought. Keep it together. Don't lose it now. Even Captain Wong said we could do this. But, it was so very dark and I truly could not see where I was going.

Suddenly, it was as though things were happening in slow motion. "The boots, the boots, check out the boots!" one of the RTOs called in. "Check out the boots! Check out the boots!" he repeated. Indeed, I had been looking down and at the boots of McCabe as he walked in front of me. I had been looking for several moments. In addition, I had also looked at the boots of the man in front of McCabe, along with the man in front of him, all of whom, at this very moment, had been marching with a mysterious glow around their boots.

The transmissions continued but I was afraid to respond to them, as I did not want anyone to think I might be losing my mind. I immediately turned to the captain to see if he was observing the same thing.

"I see the glow," he commented. "I don't know what to make of it. Notify the platoons to keep their heads down and their eyes on the boots in front of them. Dave, it's okay, we'll get through this."

I think this was the first time Captain Wong called me by my first name. Without pursuing what could have been an endless line of questioning, I placed calls to all the platoons.

"Do you see the glow?" I asked. Although the responses varied, they were all in the affirmative. First platoon RTO: "Yup. Don't know what it is but we've got the glow." Second platoon RTO: "Can't read the Times with this light but we can see who's in front and damn well see where we're going!" Third platoon RTO: (my platoon) "Mac, maybe J.C.'s looking out for us. We're cool. We can see."

I thought, what was this all about? What was happening to us? Looking up I could observe through a partial opening in the cloud, one particular star that stood out from all the rest. Whatever light the star was generating seemed to have a direct effect on the luminosity that surrounded our boots. As a cloud passed under this star, the glow would diminish but not disappear. When the cloud moved away, remarkably, the glow would intensify. We continued to march in near-total darkness, piloted by the unfettered radiance that encompassed our boots. It was a little before 5 AM when the captain, having spoken to one of his guides, gave orders for the company to halt, dismount and relax. Dutifully, LPs were established around our perimeter. Thankfully, daylight was working its way in. The early morning sky was clear. Having arrived at our new location, we were safe and unharmed. With the exception of aching bodies and sore feet, fortunately, on this particular mission there were no instances of friendly-fire.

Surprisingly, no one talked about the boots. I couldn't say for sure what truly happened to us on this particular mission. What I do know about the past many hours was the ingredients for a potentially serious mishap were abundant, and yet, we were spared from harm. And if you believe in fate, well then perhaps what took place on this particular night was nothing more and nothing less than what was supposed to have taken place.

As I looked around I caught a glimpse of one of the new guys who seemed to have an expression of wonderment as he stared off into the direction where we had just come. Curious to see what had so captured his imagination, I stood up and walked over to him.

"Is that it?" he said to me with a mid-western accent. "I never have seen one before, ya know. Why can't I hear noth'n?" he questioned.

"You will," I responded as I stared out into the direction he was looking. "I'd say soon. It takes awhile, you know, for sound to travel that distance. You can feel the ground, though. Feel the vibration?" It was just about then when the roaring thunderous sound connected with the intoxicatingly powerful image.

I observed only one other B-52 strike before. They were, as was the one I now witnessed, an unforgettably awesome sight. I watched the columns of black, white and gray smoke, as they slowly spiraled upwards, covering an area the size of several football fields.

I felt good, I thought to myself. It was good to be alive. Perhaps it was fate that allowed me to be standing where I was at that very moment. But I couldn't help reflecting, for others, destiny had come to a dreadfully different conclusion at the end of the path from which we had just come.

During World War II, in a speech to Parliament, Sir Winston Churchill was quoted as saying, "The tragedy of war is that it takes man's best to do man's worst." After a twenty-four hour stand down where we were able to shower, get some rest and unwind, Bravo Company was given orders to be airlifted in and do a sweep of the area that had been targeted by the B-52s. Jumping off the helicopter and standing only a matter of a few feet from where the first of the many bombs had fallen, I was able to fully comprehend what Churchill meant.

Trees were obliterated. Dirt, as far as you could see, that only forty-eight hours earlier had contained moisture and organisms, plants and vegetation, was burnt to a fine gray powered ash. A burning odor and a smoky haze filled the entire area. Life of any form was virtually nonexistent with a few exceptions. Every few hundred feet or so you could see the skeletal remains of what appeared to have been vegetation or possibly a tree. There were also survivors. If you had the misfortune of brushing up against any of the lifeless branches or tree limbs scattered about, you would be covered and attacked by an army of red ants.

What had started only a few days before as a repetitively routine combat ambush mission had turned out to be anything but. Or was it? After all, was this not just a game that was being played out? True, the steadfast endurance of the men of B Company, 1/27 Infantry, under the leadership of Captain Wong, had come through without the loss of any of their people. Yet, at any given time, a different hand could have been dealt. Tables could have been reversed. The key to survival in jungle warfare seemed to be not so much knowing how to play the game, as much as it was just to be able to stay in it.

8:00 PM April 12th, 1969

April 1969

Dearest David,

You're an uncle. Cyetta gave birth today. He has your name. David Cooke McCormick. She's doing fine but your brother Dennis was very nervous. The weather has been beautiful here this week...

Love,

The Mother

PS– Walk on the sidewalk

Actually, it was 7:55 PM that I first noticed him. But it was on a Saturday and on the 12th of April that he died. To be sure, it was only a five-minute difference, but it was something I had to do. It was also something I wanted to do. Above all, it was something I needed to do. Five minutes. That's all it was. Five minutes, where I ignored my duties and my responsibilities. Five minutes, during which time I shut out the world and all its surroundings. Five minutes, when I turned my back on the war and placed it on hold. Five minutes, where I talked to him and touched him and pretended he was alive.

If you asked me to tell you the type of mission we were conducting on that Saturday afternoon in the province of Binh Duong, I would be at a loss. But as the day rolled on, that would change, and change very dramatically. What was so different about the events that were to unfold was the man himself. He had an unusual first name, a name I only remembered reading about in my history class. His last name, consisting of two words, was also curious and one I had not ever heard of before. The nickname he was given was the more acceptable of the names and was the one he seemed most comfortable with. And that was "Doc." Or, if you wanted to be completely formal,

71

Specialist 4th Class, Miles D. Touchberry, Jr. He was our company medic.

He was a very peaceful and ordinary fellow whose demeanor had a sort of backwoods flavor to it. Yet he carried with him a charm and a gentlemanly manner that paid homage to all Southerners. "Well, Mac, how are things with you today?" he might quip. And when you least expected it he would mesmerize you with a pleasing sense of humor that was amusingly dry. When he did tell a joke, a sparkle in his eye revealed pleasure that exposed satisfaction from within. He was from South Carolina and lived in the small town of Sumter. He was also a C.O. (Conscientious Objector), one not willing to take another's life.

I had met and come to know a few C.O.s during my tour of duty. It wasn't long before you became aware of who was legit and who was not. A good number of soldiers claimed this status thinking this would be an automatic reprieve of combat duty. Obviously not true. But Miles was different. He was a sincere and genuine bona fide conscientious objector. From mind to body to soul, he was regimented in his belief against the taking of a human life. "Besides," he would often quip with his southern drawl, "if I injured someone I then would have the added responsibility of patching them up. You guys have it easy. All you have to worry about is shooting people!"

Although liked and respected by the members of Bravo Company, he did create a hint of discord among some of the officers and platoon leaders. Doc's strong and deep-seated convictions about not wanting to take another's life did get him into trouble. Namely, he refused to carry a weapon. This was against all Army regulations. There were, of course, times when he was ordered to carry one. In such cases he would lug one slung backwards with the barrel facing down. This was far removed from combat readiness. A few times he was even spotted with a Colt .45 pistol. It was always questionable whether any of the weapons Doc was ordered to carry contained live ammunition. But this was Doc. This was his belief. He took a position — and he maintained the fortitude and the courage to stand by it. It took me a while but I came to realize you could only admire someone like that.

He was reluctant to talk about his personal life. I did learn a little about his parents and the fact they were more like grandparents since there was a great age difference. There were times he did tell stories of life back home. The interesting thing about Miles and the stories he told was, when he got to the punch line, he didn't just pause, he took a vacation. The one thing that stood out the most was the comments he made to John Paxson and me on the evening of April 11. It was a little before 5 PM. John and I sat cleaning our weapons in preparation for the next day's mission. Miles had taken a reprieve from the ever-constant readiness and the daily activities that go on within the confines of the medical tent. Sitting down between the two of us, he started in.

"I'm ticked!" Miles proclaimed.

"What is it now, Doc?" John asked as if Doc complained on a regular basis.

"According to "the bear" (Colonel Bradley), my life is worth a minus one hundred points."

"What the heck are you talking about?" John asked, giving Doc his undivided attention.

"Well, there's a contest going on that the colonel started and the rules are that starting tomorrow, any enemy killed by us is worth fifty points," Doc said, then continued. "And the company that gets the most points over the next few weeks will be entitled to a 48-hour stand down in Vung Tau."

"Sounds good to me," John said, then added, "so what are you ticked at?"

To which Doc responded, "Well the rules go on to explain that for every one of us that is killed you must deduct one hundred points. So what the Army is telling me is, that if I am killed tomorrow, my life is worth a negative one hundred points. Now, you tell me, is that fair?" John and I continued cleaning our weapons while enjoying a brief laugh at Doc's dark humor comments. In less than twenty-four hours time, United States Army Specialist Miles D. Touchberry, Jr., would be lying dead at my feet.

In jungle warfare not all missions had tidy objectives. Sometimes we would be sent into an area where military intelligence had reports on enemy activity. Other times you would just march and wander and march, looking and searching for that one little trace of the enemy. An encounter with the enemy was always a hit-or-miss thing. Going one, two, or three days in the sultry climate without sign or sighting of our adversaries and your reflexes and focus fragment. On this twelfth day of April the members of Bravo Company strode within yards of a series of neatly camouflaged and well-fortified NVA bunkers.

There were signs of the enemy. Footprints, several dozens of them crisscrossed each of the various paths we marched down. All were fresh. Some were not even hours old. Villagers, who by daylight would ordinarily be working the fields or tending to their water buffalo and other animals were noticeably absent. The first indication of things not being right was a radio call from one of the third platoon's RTO. We were on the ground, not more than an hour or so after being ferried in by helicopter, and his comments were short and to the point: "I don't like this, I don't like this one bit."

His name was Alan Hicks and he was from the state of Nebraska. When he first came on line back in January, he was given a choice between two assignments: walking point (where you walk alone a hundred feet or more in front of the company for the purpose of detecting and giving early warning of enemy ambush), or carrying the platoon's radio. He selected the radio. With the name of Hicks and being from the mid-west he sometimes took a bit of ribbing. But he had a wonderful disposition and was the type who took things in stride. He was also a good RTO and an excellent communicator. Having a level head, he was the type you wanted to be around if things got sticky. But there was also something else about Hicks I admired from afar and yet could never fully understand. Call it mid-western corn-fed intuition, but he seemed to have a sixth sense about him. When Hicks said he didn't like something, you could be fairly sure there was something out there not to be liked. I relayed Alan's message to Captain Wong.

After several short communications and consultations between the captain, Hicks and Chico (Lt. Sanchez, the 3rd platoon leader), Captain Wong had some grave concerns. He, too, had a sense things were not right. Soon after, several members from the 1st and 2nd platoons reported what they thought to be enemy movement off in the distance within the thickly wooded area. On two separate occasions, the scout dog that was assigned to us postured in an alert position. Tension was mounting. Along with his location, RTO Hicks once again radioed in his concerns. Captain Wong was now facing a precariously serious dilemma. And it wasn't just the enemy he had to worry about.

Listening intently as the captain called out orders, I observed his facial features, I studied his mannerisms. Being around him as much as I was, I knew his body language better than most in the field. He remained calm, he stayed focused. Yet every fiber of Captain Wong's body was telling him to pull back. Ordinarily, being the commander of an infantry company, it would take just one quick order. Pull back! He'd done it before. He'd ordered regrouping for the purpose of tactical advantage. He knew how to reach his objectives with minimal casualty loss. He was the captain of Bravo Company. He was the commander. However, during these harrowing moments and on this twelfth day of April 1969, he was not in charge. Orders filtering down from a light observation helicopter hovering above dictated the fate of the events that were to unfold. On this particular mission, Captain Wong, like any good soldier, was just following directives.

United States Army Major Holiday was his name. His transportation of choice was the LOCH (light observation carrying helicopter). From there and a good distance away, he maintained a respectable overview of ground activity. He also thought he could replicate the innermost thinking of the enemy combatant. Unfortunately, on this mission, the members of Bravo Company would have been better served if the major's LOCH had been grounded.

"Mac, tell the captain that Chico spotted what appears to be several more bunkers ten to fifteen meters up and it doesn't look good," RTO Hicks radioed from up forward. I was really feeling for Hicks. His radio antenna made him a prime target and yet he was maintaining steady and constant communications with me. Captain Wong wanted to heed the warnings and strategically regroup. From the air, it would appear Major Holiday wanted us to confront the enemy within his time frame. The major's orders were to the point and unmistakably clear. We were to continue forward and close in on the enemy. Holiday's directives did not just supercede Wong's authority, they also forced Wong to downplay his instincts. Captain Wong basically had his hands tied. Grabbing my handset, the captain called into Hicks, "The orders are to move forward, what can I say? Use extra caution, do you roger that? Use extra caution!" The tension in Hicks voice was plainly noticeable as he whispered back to me, "Holiday should be on the ground on this one. Maybe then…" He had yet to release the transmit key on his radio when the enemy opened fire. The initial stages of battle came across and into my handset with deafening sounds. The NVAs were well equipped, including numerous automatic machine guns. The fighting was intense.

Chico was first to be hit. Soon after was M-60 machine gun operator Specialist 4th class Michael Smith, age twenty. He died instantly after taking a bullet to the heart. Eyewitness accounts reported seeing blood from a severed artery shoot almost three feet into the air. From a half dozen exploding enemy grenades, RTO Alan Hicks was next to be hit. Crawling up behind Hicks in an effort to assess the situation and ward off the enemy, Lt. Stamatios Alexander took a bullet between the eyes. He died instantly. With the firefight in full force, Specialist 4th class Daniel Hughes (our company tunnel rat from Keosanqua, Iowa), under concentrated fire heroically maneuvered forward with much needed munitions. Although making more than one supply run, Hughes would remain unharmed.

The transmissions were coming in at a lightning pace. Being on the listening end of the many calls, I realized some of our people were dying only a short distance forward of us. For the briefest of moments I was frightened. You might even say terrified. But being in the command center, where information is filtered and orders are given, you have no time to lament. The feelings I had were it was someone else's time to go and, thankfully, at least for this moment, it was not my turn. With these thoughts came a peace and security from within that held me together and assisted me in maintaining my focus on the commands Captain Wong shouted out.

There were many others who were hit during the initial stages of the battle, but I was most concerned about Hicks. Our command center was approximately 150 feet back, yet we may just as well have been in Timbuktu. RTO Alan Hicks was our eyes and our ears. Without him we were blind. Over the next few minutes, Alan communicated in a clear and precise manner a steady stream of situation reports, which allowed Captain Wong to exercise the judgment needed to fend off the enemy attack. But the very last transmission that came across my handset threw me off guard. "Oh, and by the way," Alan nonchalantly commented, "I've been hit and I'm down."

Lying wounded, out in the open and without the basics of cover, RTO Hicks was determined to maintain the flow of communications he knew was necessary. His last call would be at 5:55 PM. A bullet fired from a nearby bunker sliced its way into Alan's handset as he was about to make a call. It shattered into several pieces. Miraculously, though the handset was only inches from his head, the bullet spared the fallen RTO. It did, however, sever communications, communications that were the lifeline of the company. The bullet not only destroyed the handset, it also keyed in and transmitted a dead signal, disabling all communications between our command center and everyone else.

Within moments, the second of the 3rd platoon's RTOs, Ken Sikes from Glendale, Arizona, under heavy fire, low crawled over to Hicks to see about restoring radio communications. Coming up behind Hicks and seeing the shattered handset, Ken Sikes was now exposed to the opening in the enemy bunker and the machine gun that lay within. As he looked directly into the bunker not more than 50 feet away, a horrendous fear encompassed his entire being, a fear so great it would lead him to believe this would be the very spot where he would die. A fear, so overpowering, that within a short period of time would lead the twenty-year-old Sikes to succumb to and accept his very own death. But this sense of mortality would be short-lived. Even as the machine gun fired away, a sensation of calm and peace was slowly developing from within. His earlier acceptance of death led him to and created a sensation of tranquility that he never before experienced. At 6:05 PM, RTO Ken Sikes would lean in front of Alan, disconnect the damaged handset, and do a change in frequencies that would restore communications with the command center and the other platoons. Sikes, lying flat on his stomach, whose only protection was from a small growth of shrubbery, was now in steady communication with Captain Wong, relaying situation reports as they occurred.

Meanwhile Doc sitting nearby and almost on top of one of the well-camouflaged bunkers, witnessed Alan's injuries. In an effort to render aid he made a quick dash to his side. In doing so, Doc knowingly and very gallantly ran out into the field of fire. Reaching the injured Hicks, Doc failed to do what he was trained to do. He did not look at, nor did he take the time to access his patient's injuries. He did not attempt to immediately administer first aid as he was taught to do. Instead, despite the fact bullets were flying everywhere, Doc took the precious few moments necessary to unhook and unstrap the non-functioning radio that was attached to Alan's back. Completing this maneuver, he very strategically placed the radio alongside Alan's head in an effort to give cover and protect his charge from further injuries.

On this particular day, Doc was not carrying a side arm. The only protection he had was the medical insignia that was clearly displayed on both his carry bags, an insignia that is understood and recognized internationally. This did not seem to deter the enemy. Taking careful aim from within a nearby bunker, a shot rang out piercing the topside of the radio that was now protecting Alan's head. Both escaped injury. More bullets were fired. Leaning over the wounded radiotelephone operator in an attempt to administer aid and at the same time protect his charge, Miles D. Touchberry, Jr. took one of the bullets to the chest. Before the fighting stopped, darkness would settle in.

"Only 'Whiskeys' (wounded) to the LZ. All 'Kilos' (killed) at my feet," I shouted into the handset in an attempt to be heard, as the first of the medical helicopters was beginning its descent. Although a commonsense command, it was important enough to repeat several times, especially for the newer people. In the confusion of a battle or firefight, it is easy for you to be eager to get someone that was killed onto the first available medevac. This is particularly true if the one lying dead was someone you had gotten to know or someone you were close to. An unpleasant part of my job was prioritizing who goes and who stays. Space aboard a medevac is a valuable commodity and at times quite limited.

A little before 8 PM the bodies began arriving at my location. I had been standing near a large fallen tree, communicating with the medevac as the first stretcher was placed down at my feet. The glow from some of our tracer bullets, seen from the air, prompted the pilot to ask if the landing zone was secure. I lifted my foot and gently touched the bottom left corner of the stretcher where a body lay uncovered as I responded back in the affirmative. For numerous reasons I delayed looking down. At the same time I was keenly focused on my communications with the pilot, talking him down and guiding him in. Look down, look down, Dave, and see who it is, a voice was saying in the back of my mind. The fighting had died down considerably, however, from the noise coming across the airwaves, it sounded more intense. The pilot seemed a bit hesitant in making his landing. Two more bodies were deposited at my feet. Several ambulatory were stationed at the landing zone awaiting evacuation. About a dozen more stretcher cases and seriously wounded were being lined up and awaiting evacuation.

The helicopter had now completed its touchdown. Although I had been putting it off, it was now my time, my time to look down. With what little light there was my eye contact was precise and deliberate. It was the boots I saw first. They were dirty and well-worn. Dave, I said to myself, this is not someone new in country. This is someone who has been around for a while, someone you probably know. Okay, I'm okay, I thought. I've done this many times before. It's no big deal. Suddenly, the ground area exploded with illumination as a helicopter, hovering above, directed its powerful spotlight down upon us. My eyes quickly shifted to survey his jungle fatigues. Older, faded, and without the slightest hint of a crease. All right Dave, this is gonna be someone you know, so let's get it over with, I contemplated. But wait, there was something very unusual about these fatigues. Many of the pockets were stuffed with ace bandages. There was blood on his chest, yet fresh gauze and medical dressings were stuffed in his pockets. For an instant I wondered why Doc would have placed these medical supplies in this dead person's pockets. Wait a minute, I hadn't heard from Doc since the firefight broke out. My eyes were still set on the fatigues. No, I thought, don't let this be Miles. Don't let this be Doc.

My concentration was broken as the medevac pilot radioed, "Charlie Papa, we have touched down and can take two litters and four ambulatory, do you copy? Over!" The spotlight from the passing helicopter had spun away and on to another area but not before I was able to catch a glimpse of the young soldier's face. It was as if I had just been punched in the stomach. Every measure of breath from within me had taken its leave. I allowed my handset, the lifeline of the company, to just drop and dangle to my side. The sixty some odd pounds of weight from the radio and my supplies seemed to work in unison as the strength in my legs gave way. I dropped to my knees only a matter of inches from his head. "Doc," I whispered. "Oh no, not you, Doc, not you," I repeated. "You're a CO, they couldn't have hit you."

I saw a peaceful look on his face. His eyes were shut and it appeared almost as if he were asleep. The light from the helicopter splashed down upon us once more. From the dangling handset I could hear, but did not respond to the medevac pilot, as he called out to me, "Charlie Papa, we are ready to receive up to four ambulatory and two litters, do you copy? Over" I stared at Miles for what seemed to be an eternity. I then took the back of my hand and did what I could to remove the dirt and grime from the day's encounter. Slowly I rubbed it alongside the right portion of his cheek. No, not you Doc, not you, you're a CO, I repeated in my head.

My dazed condition was suddenly broken by John Paxson who, in a state of disbelief, called out, "Is that Doc, is that Touch?" I looked up and over my shoulder at John. The roar of the helicopter engine made normal conversation all but impossible to understand. "He was a CO, John, a God damn CO, that's not right, that's just not right," I said in a natural tone, making a conscious effort not to shout over Doc's body and not really caring if John heard me or not.

"Charlie Papa, Charlie Papa, this is Cobra 298, we have a moving target just outside of your grid in location K32, K33, request permission to open fire," a pilot of a Cobra gunship radioed into me. I did not respond. Once more, he repeated his message. Once again, I failed to answer.

Pushing my handset away and straining to reach around my back, I unfastened the release clips that secured my knapsack. Reaching inside I yanked out my poncho liner and shook it briskly until it was in the full opened position. Once again another call, "Charlie Papa, this is Medevac Two, we are in route and should be arriving your location in about zero-three (three minutes). Understand you have one medevac on the ground, is that affirm?" Once again I shirked my responsibilities as command RTO, I did not respond. Carefully I wrapped the lower section of the liner around Doc's feet, tucking and securing it. I then pulled the liner up to and under his chin, making a deliberate effort to avoid covering his head. Echoing out of the dangling handset were the numerous and continuing calls from the various helicopter pilots. So, very gently I patted Doc on the side of his face. You'll be okay, I feigned to myself; you'll be okay.

Jumping to my feet I caught the attention of two new recruits as they were hurrying by. "You two," I shouted out, "get this litter over to the medevac."

"But I thought orders were…" one of them started to say as I sharply interrupted. "Shut the fuck up and get him over to the chopper now, you hear me? Now!" Reaching down and grabbing my handset I was immediately besieged by non-stop transmissions. Regaining my composure, and checking with the captain, I took control and filtered the calls one by one.

"Cobra 298, this is Charlie Papa, you are authorized to fire on all areas excluding grids K18 through 20. I repeat, excluding grids K18 through 20, friendlies on the ground, please re-confirm before firing."

The Cobra pilot instantly responded, "Roger, Charlie Papa, all areas excluding grids K18 through K20," then added, "Are we good with your frequency? We've been trying you for five minutes"

"Roger, frequency fine," I answered and continued, "Air-born medevacs, the LZ is secure and you are clear to land in Grid K19. Be advised, use caution, you have one medevac on the ground who will be departing shortly. Please acknowledge."

Working my communications with the various pilots I stood and watched as the two recruits placed Doc's body down next to two other litters that had just been examined and were in the process of being lifted inside the medevac. Three litters I thought, they can handle three litters. In addition and as requested, four ambulatory, with an assortment of wounds were standing in front awaiting evacuation. One by one, the on-board medic assisted them inside. Go, Doc, go, I murmured to myself, you'll be okay. Two of the ambulatory were now seated inside. The pilot of the second medevac, requesting to be talked down, broke my concentration. As he hovered overhead, I did my best to point out and identified the location of the secondary staging area, which contained more wounded. The pilot, somewhat concerned the staging area was too close to the first medevac, asked the wounded be moved back a bit.

While radioing these instructions to the RTO at the secondary staging area, I watched as the medic was now ready to make a quick examination of Doc. Come on, get him on board I whispered to myself, while breaking my communication with the RTO. Briefly the medic shined a flashlight onto Doc's face, then into his eyes. For a good period of time he explored with his hands, feeling for a sign, any sign that might signify life, searching for the pulse that was so successful in eluding him. Doing my best to contain my emotions and not taking my eyes off the medic, I transmitted new landing instructions to the pilot of the second medevac. Halfway through my directions the medic who had been examining Doc reached down, grabbed the two sides of the poncho liner and pulled it up and over Doc's head. Immediately after the medic jumped to his feet. While preparing to board the helicopter, he turned and stared in my direction and, for one brief moment, shook his head ever so slightly. Then, climbing aboard and grabbing the handle, he slid the door shut.

With my handset pressed hard against my ear I waited and listened for the medic or the pilot to say something, anything, about Doc. Seconds ticked by while he sat on the ground. Then the sound of the pilot's voice, "Charlie Papa, this is Medevac one,...we are set to lift off,...be advised we are a little bit top heavy,...understand we are leaving one Kilo on the ground. Med two or three coming in now should be able to accommodate him." I was not able to respond to the transmission. I was too consumed in trying to accept the fact my friend Miles was gone. Staring out at the stretcher, where his body lay covered, I thought of the terrible irony of the situation. He was there to help. Truly, he was one of the good guys.

In war, I thought, there is a saying your best and only friend is your weapon. If that is the case, then a soldier's second best friend is his poncho liner (blanket). It can warm you at night and camouflage you by day. It was the soldier's security blanket and something that was in great demand. I have heard of their being stolen. I had seen soldiers fighting over them. I had even seen some pay money just for an extra. With rare exception, a soldier never gave his poncho liner away. I felt comfort in the fact my liner was covering Doc's body.

As the engines whined and began to build up force, the propeller's spin created powerful gusts of wind blasting a torrent of warm air all about. With each rotation of the blades the wind grew stronger and more forceful. Looking down and to the side of the medevac, I watched as my poncho liner covering Doc's body began to flutter in the artificial winds, gently at first, then, after a moment, with an infuriating vigor. Within seconds the liner covering Doc's body began to unravel, first unfastening at his feet, then with lift-off all but inevitable, blowing free of his body. Almost as if in slow motion, the green and brown and tan color collage of work that made up the ever so popular liner began to float up and down and all around. Suddenly the liner was drawn up and pulled into the rapidly spinning blades, where it shredded like papier-mâché into a hundred thousand miniscule pieces. Staring in awe, the battle weary survivors of Bravo Company, some standing, some kneeling, some lying down, brought, for the briefest of moments, all activities to a halt, as what remained of the liner showered down upon them. At that moment, I knew my friend Miles was gone.

GETTING PINNED

May 1969

Dearest David,

Not a good week here. Had to have "Katie" put to sleep. She was a good dog and the house is so silent and lonely without her. Hope all is going well for you…

Love,

The Mother

PS– Walk on the sidewalk

"What time is it, anyway?" asked Charles Hintzen, who went by his father's nickname of "Hatch" and was standing directly behind me.

"My Seiko says 12:40," I answered, "but I wouldn't go by that. I bought it off a village boy a few days ago and I could swear that it's snowing inside the dial."

"Snow in the dial?" Hatch quipped, then added, "Then it's not a Seiko." Hatch was a character, a likable fellow who was never without a comeback line. He was from the tougher side of Patterson in the state of New Jersey. Although not a mean-spirited person, his one-liners were rarely without sarcasm. He was also on line considerably longer than most and had gone through, taken part in and witnessed a lot more battles. The sarcasm was nothing more than a defense mechanism, I thought.

We were at the start of a forty-eight hour stand-down back in Cu Chi. Over the next few days our time would be our own. For those of us who didn't step out of line, there would be no authority to answer to. It all seemed so surreal. Only hours earlier we were slapping mosquitoes and wiping sweat as we sliced our way through jungle brush that brought us to the end of a two-week ambush mission. Now, the entire company, standing in formation, was stationed outside of headquarters. It was a mystery why we were here, standing at ease with dirt on our bodies and mud on our fatigues. There was an obvious thrill and excitement in the air with the prospect of time off, or, as we jokingly referred to it, time out. As I looked up and down the rows of men, I began to run through my mind some of the things I needed to take care of and wanted to do before our next mission. Batteries, socks, T-shirts and some canned fruit. Also, I needed to remember to get a new radio antenna as I had taken a fall and broken it last month and had been using my backup ever since. I also wanted to visit my friend Ronnie, from Yonkers, who had somehow finagled himself off line and was now stationed here in Cu Chi.

The sun was shining brightly, and, for the first time in a long while, the temperature and humidity were comfortable. A colonel accompanied by two aides approached the company. An order was shouted out snapping us all to attention. "Award of the Bronze Star Medal with V device, for Heroism under fire in connection with military operations against a hostile force. Specialist McCormick, David W. US55527434 distinguished himself by heroic actions...." Wait just one moment, I reflected. No, no, no, this is just not right. I don't deserve this medal. Don't they know? They must have known. I was always open and obvious about the whole situation. I told the captain. It was just a routine mission. I don't deserve this medal. I don't. As the aide continued to spout forth these heroic actions, my mind took flight to that eventful morning.

"Charlie Papa, Charlie Papa, be advised Duke has stopped, I say again, Duke has stopped," came the radioed transmission, garbled with static, from the lead platoon's RTO. I had only known Duke for approximately six weeks. Yet, during that short period of time, I had fallen in love with him. He was a handsome fellow, with dark hair and beautiful brown eyes. He was on special assignment and had been out with us on several missions. He was exceptionally good at spotting and tracking enemy movement. He also had four paws, and as usual was leading point. He and his handler, Joe Aylmer from Philadelphia, were made for each other and not ones to take chances. They were assigned to Bravo Company on our last three missions. In each case, Duke and Joe alerted and gave our company early and advance notice of the location of enemy ambush sites, giving us a distinct tactical advantage for the purpose of defending and attacking.

Joe worked closely with the platoon's RTO. The RTO on this mission was relatively new but someone who had excellent communication skills. His name was Tom Donovan, and he was quick to relay in an accurate and precise manner the necessary warnings the handler would pass on to him. Although Donovan was with our company only for a short period of time, I had my eye on him. He had good potential for my position as the captain's RTO, which could be my ticket off line.

The first time I broached the subject of carrying the captain's radio to Donovan, his feelings were purely apprehensive.

"Isn't the captain the primary target on any ambush mission?" queried Donovan. This bothered me a little as I felt he was too new to be asking such questions. "Well, yes, I guess so," I responded. I immediately realized my response might not have gotten me the results I desired. I also made a mental note to be sure, if I ever get out of this mess, I would avoid anything that might be sales related.

"Well, then, wouldn't it go without saying that the captain's RTO is the second primary target on any ambush mission?" Donovan inquired. Damn, he had me on that, I thought.

"Well, yes, okay, that may be a downside, but the position does come with a number of perks," I feebly retorted.

We went back and forth on this matter for a number of weeks. I threw every benefit I could come up with at him. I told him by carrying the captain's radio you didn't have to carry any extra supplies. You didn't always have to pull guard duty. You would be free from KP. You could request and sometimes get an extra twenty-four hour pass. You could carry your weapon of choice including a .45. You wouldn't have to take any crap from anyone. And, best of all, you'd always be the first to know what was going on at all times throughout the company. I did feel some of this did pique his interest, but he still was not totally sold on the idea of carrying the captain's radio. Then one evening, after a harrowing daytime firefight, I was prepared to make my closing arguments to him. We both were a little on edge as his platoon and my platoon took the brunt of an ambush earlier on. However, we both worked in harmony as we called in extra firepower. I was impressed with how he assisted in communicating and coordinating fire from the hovering Cobra gunship, thus allowing me to call in the necessary medevacs for the wounded.

I approached Donovan as he was changing batteries on his radio. I had rehearsed what I wanted to say to him and was direct and to the point.

"Tom," I asked, "why did you join the Army?"

"What kind of question is that? I got drafted like everybody else," he quipped without looking up from his radio. The light from the evening stars glimmered down upon his face, displaying a softness that made him appear to be much younger than his 20 years.

"Well, I mean after you were drafted, you had a choice. You could have picked another branch such as Air Force or Navy or Coast Guard," I said.

"No way "José," any one of those would have been an additional two years. You know that. I am not wasting two more years of my life. I just wanted to get in and out and get on with my life as quickly as possible," he replied. Got him, I thought!

"Okay, then listen up," I said. "Officers don't spend more than six months on line. It's a little like they're somewhat of a god. The upper brass feels that anything more than six months on line for an officer is like a punishment or something. If you carry the captain's radio, you're sure to be in tight with him. You can then request and probably get an off line position when the captain is transferred. That's only six months on line. Think about that."

"Yeah, but wait a minute. You've been on line more than six months," Donovan challenged.

"That's correct, but not always as the captain's RTO," I responded, then added, "Look, Captain Wong is gonna be transferred soon and I'm gonna ask to go with him. But they won't transfer me without an experienced and acceptable company RTO. That's a fact. Now, if you're interested, I can speak to the captain. If not, then I'm gonna ask Sikes or Hicks" (other RTOs). Without responding he continued to work on the radio. I stood up and began to walk away when he called out, "You think I can handle it?" After a brief pause that ended with a silent thank you prayer to God, I turned to Donovan and said, "You can handle it."

The next morning as the company prepared for another day of a search and destroy mission, I told Captain Wong I had yet to take an

R & R and I was thinking of putting in for one in a few weeks. He said he would need to first take a look at future operations but if I were due the time off I would get it. He then inquired who would take over as command RTO in my absence. I told him about Donovan and that I had good vibes about him and felt he could handle the job during the week I was gone. The captain thought about it for a good moment, then said fine, sending a rush of jubilation throughout every part of my body. I did it, I actually did it. My replacement is in the wings and his name is Donovan.

"What have we got, Mac?" asked Captain Wong.

"I'm not sure yet, but Duke just went on the alert again," I responded. The captain grabbed my handset and radioed the forward platoon.

"Put the handler on," the captain ordered, somewhat perturbed. This was the fourth time within an hour Duke's actions warranted his handler to stop the company and place us on alert.

"What's going on up there?" demanded the captain as he spoke to the handler.

"I'm not sure, sir," responded Joe. "Duke's in the alert position and senses something off in the far right wood line."

"Could he have spotted an animal or something? I mean, we're making no head-way and you can't be stopping the company every fifteen minutes," the captain exclaimed.

"All I can tell you is that Duke is trained to spot movement. He also has an excellent sense of smell. And he either saw something or he smelled something and he is still in the alert position, sir," Joe responded, somewhat annoyed.

"Okay, we'll hold here for a moment and I'm coming up front," said the captain.

The time was 11:40 AM. With my handset pinned to my ear I followed Captain Wong forward until the handler and dog were in sight. As we got closer, we could plainly see Duke was indeed in the alert position. He was frozen in place with head pointing forward, tail extended nearly straight back. He looked as if he was about to leap out at something, yet except for a few small mounds of dirt along with several dried-out bushes you could plainly see through, there was nothing visibly in sight. Standing next to Joe was Donovan.

Captain Wong, sensing something was not right, told me to have Joe and Duke pull back and position themselves in a more secure area behind our platoon. He did this with good reason. The dog handler's mission was to spot and alert, not to do battle. I radioed ahead to Donovan who was only a few hundred feet in front and asked him to put Joe on the line. Sensing a little tension in the air, my humor took over.

"Joe, be advised the captain wants Duke to move behind the lines for his own safety. However, it is okay for you to remain forward out in the open without cover," I said jokingly. Joe and I had spent several late nights together downing beers back in Dau Tieng. He would constantly talk of his home life back in Philadelphia and about how he was going to purchase the new automobile called an Opal GT. He bent the rules against outsiders socializing with the dogs by allowing me to hang out with Duke. It brought back fond memories of home and our family's dog, named Katie. Knowing my sense of humor, Joe just shook his head as he directed Duke to turn back with him towards the safety of our newly established front line.

What no one realized at the time was the mound of dirt, looking so plain and natural was in fact an enemy bunker. The burst of enemy rifle fire took us all by surprise. It seemed to be coming from one location, and that was the mound of dirt several hundred feet ahead and to the right, the very direction Duke was alerting us to. The bullets flew by in several short bursts, and although Duke had done everything he could, short of a verbal warning, to point out a potential hazard, we were all caught off guard. I was standing in front of a shallow trench, which I immediately dove for. Captain Wong followed and landed alongside of me. For a moment there was absolute silence. Then Captain Wong poked his head up to scope out the situation. I was lying on my back on top of my radio. In life threatening situations such as this, thoughts of preservation seemed to supersede my responsibilities as RTO. My M-16 was locked and loaded, the safety catch off. I was ready to do battle. Then, from what sounded like the same location, came a second burst of fire. This one was longer than before, clearly the familiar sounds of the AK-47.

"Give me the radio," Captain Wong called out in his most authoritative manner. "There's a bunker about 50 meters out where the firing appears to be coming from. We've got a man down out front." He radioed the second platoon to see if they had a better perspective of the overall situation. I popped my head up to see who had been hit.

"Stay down!" the captain yelled in a state of anger he had not before shown to me. But it was too late. As I pulled myself back down to the safety of our cover, I had already seen what I had to see, a man down out in front, lying flat on his stomach, equally distant between the enemy bunker and us. His right arm was extended and embraced the top of his helmet. His left arm was stretched down his lower body and clamped around his ankle. But that wasn't the sight that grabbed my attention. The vision that stayed with me was of the equipment he was carrying. A radio. He was an RTO. It could only have been Donovan.

Several seconds later, I could hear the pained voice of Donovan calling out, "I've been hit! I've been hit! I can't move. Oh Jesus, I've been hit." Lying on my back and listening to his cries was as if my entire life was flashing by me. Yet for the moment, all I could think of was lying out there in the wide-open field was my one and only ticket off line. It was as if the entire world had just crumbled down upon me, and for one miniscule second I experienced the hopeless feeling that exists when you hit absolute rock bottom.

Clinging to whatever hope that remained within me, I did what I could to refocus my thoughts. There's one of my RTOs not more than two hundred feet from me who had been shot and is now lying out in the open with no cover or protection. If someone doesn't do something, anything, and soon, the next volley of fire may be aimed at him. I thought back to a story I had been told while attending college in Florida. I was never quite sure if it was true or not as I had heard differing versions from various people. It was about an automobile crash that had taken place and somehow the driver's young daughter had gotten pinned under the car, apparently in some rural area. With the likelihood of neither help nor assistance arriving anytime soon, the woman was able to lift the section of the automobile that entrapped her daughter and free her from the wreckage. True or not, it was that very story that gave me the strength, the resolve and the willpower to do what I had to do.

Not more than a minute or two had gone by from the first hail of enemy shots. Captain Wong was halfway into a sit-rep (situation report) from the other platoons. Glancing over at me, he watched as I began to unbuckle the straps that secured the radio to my back. I was on a mission. I was determined. And I would not be stopped.

"Mac!" the captain said, interrupting his radio transmission. "What's gotten into you?"

"I'm going to get Donovan," I called back, as I was halfway out of the trench. "Cover me, but please don't shoot me," I added in a witty and dry sardonic tone. I was now standing in a partially crouched position. The only thing between the enemy bunker and me was Donovan.

My focus and attention were at their absolute peak, and it was not directed at Donovan. It was glued to the enemy bunker less than 150 feet in front of me. I was running double time, arms stretched out wide, palms open, displaying to a hopefully compassionate and sympathetic enemy I was without a weapon. Minus the cumbersome burden of my radio, I felt an inner strength I had not experienced before. It seemed an eternity before making it to my destination, and, for the moment, no shots were fired from either side. Reaching the fallen Donovan, I dropped fast and hard onto the top of his body, never once, not even for a fraction of a second taking my eyes off the menacing bunker that was now no more than seventy-five feet in front of me.

"And you wanted to carry the captain's radio," I mockingly blurted out.

"Hey, McCormick, am I glad to see you," Donovan said with a grimace.

"How bad are you hit?" I asked as I unclipped the straps that secured his radio to his back.

"Got it in the leg, don't know if I can walk, you may have to carry me," he said. I knew I could carry him if I had to, but I also knew we would make an endearing target, especially since I would not be able to move fast. I reached down and placed my arm underneath his body.

Suddenly, I began feeling a strong sensation of pounding from within me. It felt so very odd. I was hoping it was just my heart from the running and the apprehension. But what I slowly began to realize was, this vibration I experienced from within was the beginning stage of fear, attempting to take over and take control. Within seconds, this element of fear was beyond knocking at my door. It had one foot in, a good hold and was pushing hard. While lying here on top of Donovan, with nothing more than thin air separating us from the enemy, the very real possibility existed, at any moment, we could be cut in two by enemy fire. It was only a short distance separating us from safety, but because of the circumstances, it could just as well have been a mile. Doing everything in my power to fight back this growing fear I allowed my sense of humor to kick in. "Where the hell's the sidewalk?" I asked of Donovan. He just looked at me with a puzzled grin.

Meanwhile I was unaware Captain Wong had given the order to hold all fire out of concern of a friendly-fire incident. He ordered everyone who had a clear and unobstructed shot at the bunker to train their weapons on it and fire only on his orders. Captain Wong felt by holding fire he would in essence be encouraging the enemy to make a run for it rather than go up against our well-fortified platoons.

Pushing the radio aside and placing my other arm around Donovan's chest, I lifted him to his feet. At the same time I was doing whatever I could to fight back the growing fears of being shot to death while assisting a fellow human being. War, I hate war.

We made it back to the trench that morning without additional shots being fired from either side. The medic attended to Donovan. Captain Wong ordered part of the first platoon to track down the retreating enemy, but to no avail. They disappeared, as usual, into the undergrowth that was part of the land they were most familiar with.

"What are you getting, the RTO push button award?" Hatch sarcastically asked, snapping me out of my trance. I don't remember Hatch being out there with us on this particular mission, but I do remember asking myself whether or not I should justly receive this award. When I first spotted Donovan lying out there in the dirt, doubled over, not knowing whether he was dead or just badly wounded, my only thoughts were of my own self-interest. Getting off line. It was *he* who was supposed to be getting *me* to safety. As I stepped forward I began to move past the row of men, one by one, all standing at attention. Making my way towards the colonel, his aide and Captain Wong, I wondered, had Donovan not been my choice, my potential ticket off line, would I have still charged out there? And do I truly deserve to wear this medal?

FIRE NOT SO FRIENDLY: LOSING MINNESOTA

June 1969

Dearest David,

Aunt Helen fell and broke her ankle but is doing well. Saw Kathy and Mrs. Morrone yesterday. Both said hello and wanted you to know you will be getting a bigger food package than the one the Leones sent.

Hope all is going as best as can be for you...

Love,

The Mother

PS – Walk on the sidewalk

This was a time of major transition for me as my teacher, my mentor, my protector and my friend, Captain Fred Wong was transferred and took a position off line with the S-2 (Intelligence). His replacement was a far cry from the quick and decisive leadership of Captain Wong. He was a young fellow who went by the book and yet seemed somehow disconnected from the men. The security, trust and chemistry I enjoyed and took for granted while serving under Captain Wong as command RTO was nonexistent with our new CO. But worse than that, after the first few missions, I got the feeling this captain did not know what he was doing.

On one mission we were on the trail of a small platoon of Vietcong. I radioed TOC headquarters and alerted them Bravo Company was tracking and on the move, which was standard operating procedure. TOC radioed back and asked for our location. I asked the captain for our grids. He seemed annoyed and snapped back, "I am not stopping the entire company just to give out grids." I radioed TOC we would get back to them shortly with our location. It was just a sense I had, but I got the impression he had no idea where we were at that particular moment. This was not a good sign. It was also something that would repeat itself with deadly consequences.

Over the course of the next few missions my concern escalated. I waited for a lull in activity, when I asked for and received permission to take a twenty-four hour leave of absence. I had gotten to a point where I no longer felt I could continue being the command RTO. All the many months of on line duty had taken their toll. I wanted off line. Staying alive in this God-forsaken country was nothing more than a crap shoot, nothing more than luck, and I did not want to be forced into a play where the odds of staying alive no longer seemed favorable. My plan was to hitch a ride back to headquarters, track down and meet privately with Captain Wong and ask him to do what he could to get me off line and away from this new CO.

The following day, with my M-16 in one hand and a knapsack packed with a clean set of fatigues in the other, I jumped a seat on one of the several convoys heading in the direction of Dau Tieng. Having spent the better part of the year fighting in the jungles and not engaged in too many missions involving convoys, I was not familiar with the everyday hazards and necessary safety procedures that were routinely followed by the drivers on these daily runs. If an enemy sniper takes a shot at a truck, it can easily throw off the pace of the convoy. If a truck breaks down, the convoy stops. If a suspicious object is spotted in the roadway, the convoy will do a slow detour. What I thought was going to be a two-hour trip had, with all stops, taken considerably longer.

When I arrived in Dau Tieng, I went directly to the division clerk's office to see about getting some food, a shower and a place to sleep for the night. I also wanted to know where I could find Captain Wong. The clerk was a former member of our third platoon and someone who recently celebrated his nineteenth birthday. After spending only six weeks on line he had claimed "battle-fatigue" and somehow schemed his way off line and into his current position. I had heard about this several months ago. His position was a relatively safe and comfortable one, with no bullets to dodge, three hot cooked meals a day, showers whenever and his own cot to sleep in at night. Not too bad, I thought. However when he told me how the company brass had him working from 7 AM to 11 PM, submitting reports, writing letters of commendation and getting out the colonel's daily "Dear Mr. and Mrs., I regret to inform you that your son was killed letters," I had to feel sympathetic.

He told me I could bunk for the night in the transfer hut located directly across the road, and I must be out by tomorrow since replacement recruits from the states would be arriving. The mess tent opened at 4 PM, I would need a pass, which would be no problem. S-2, where I could find Captain Wong, was just down the road and on the same side. Showers were located across from S-2. Tired from my trip and hoping he recognized me as the captain's RTO, I asked him if the transfer hut was the best place for me to get some rest.

"It should be quiet," he said. Then added with a wily grin, "Besides White, you'll have the entire place to yourself." White, I thought. Now that's interesting. I don't know if I care to deal with him right now.

Deciding not to wait until morning to speak to the captain, I headed down the road towards S-2. The old, one story wooden barracks-like building was heavily fortified with extra layers of sandbags on all sides. At the end of the dirt sidewalk that led up to the front screened entrance were two oil drums cut in half, painted white and used as planters. I remembered thinking the flowers were particularly vibrant and offered a stark contrast to the surrounding area. Standing guard out front with an M-16 slung over his shoulder was a heavy set but very relaxed looking sergeant.

"Can I help you, soldier?" he asked rather pleasantly.

"I was looking for Captain Wong," I responded.

"Gone for the day. Catch him first thing in the morning, 07 hundred," the sergeant said. Slightly disappointed, I figured I would do what the sergeant suggested and catch him in the morning. I headed back towards the transfer hut. Walking along the dusty, dry dirt road, I shifted my thoughts. I was no longer thinking of getting off line. I was now focused on how I was going to spend a night in the same barracks as White.

White, a member of one of our platoons, stood just a little under six-feet tall. He was remarkably good looking and had inherited his fine chiseled features from his French Canadian born parents. At the age of twenty-two, he could easily have been a cover-boy model for any one of those '60's muscle magazines. There was a captivating

95

manner about him, yet at times he appeared aloof. From a distance, I had admired White. There were times I even looked up to him. But that all came to an abrupt end a little over a month ago. That's when he became a casualty and a statistic of this very unpleasant conflict. By his own hand and with his own weapon, he calculatingly located the area between the bones of his big toe and the one next to it, placed the barrel of his M-16 to within an inch of his foot, and purposefully squeezed off one round. The wound was clean and, as he had planned, appeared to be without permanent damage. Consequently, White had met the criteria and qualified himself for the dubious label of 'SIW' (Self-Inflicted Wound), receiving a court-martial and a dishonorable discharge in exchange for safe haven and return stateside. A controversial price though it may be, it was his ticket off line.

I would be dishonest if I told you the idea of doing something like this to myself hadn't crossed my mind. In fact it had, so many times I couldn't even begin to count. When in a foxhole, and the enemy is not in sight but his mortar rounds are paced and "walking" in towards you, closer and closer, and the only cover and protection you have is from the thickness of the shirt on your back, you think about it. When diving for cover and falling on top of what's left of the guy next to you after walking head on into an ambush or being thrown by a land mine that just exploded, you think about it. Getting off line would be easy. It would take just one shot. Clean, quick and uncomplicated. Prudence, however, had been the better part of my upbringing. Besides, my tolerance for pain was in short supply. If I were to take a hit, I decided, it would be the enemy who would have to accommodate me.

As the clerk had said, with the exception of White the hut was empty. Apparently under house arrest, wearing a pair of Government Issue military green boxer shorts and an ace bandage wrapped around his right foot, there he lay off in the corner.

"Hey," I said to him with no particular excitement. Recognizing me but not remembering my name, he asked me what I was doing here. I told him I had some company business and I was here just for the night. I threw my knapsack and weapon down on a cot.

"Guess you heard about this," he said, looking down at his foot as he began to sit up. "I don't know what the fuck I was thinking. Now they're talking about keeping me here for the remainder of my tour doing KP and stuff. Can you believe that bullshit? Christ, I should have hit the bone. Then I'd have been out of here."

Only halfway listening to him, I started to undress. For the moment, I wanted nothing more than to take a long, cool shower, get some hot food in me and have a good night's sleep. Although not for protection, I decided to take my M-16 with me as I headed out to get cleaned up. I suppose I looked rather silly walking down the road with my shower kit and clean fatigues in one hand, an M-16 in the other with only a towel wrapped around my waist.

After showering and getting something to eat, I returned to the hut. White, still in his shorts, was limping around holding a bottle of beer in one hand, a wooden cane in the other. So much for house arrest, I thought. I was tired and in need of sleep. I got undressed, folded and put away the clean pair of fatigues I was wearing and laid myself down on a cot several rows distant from his. I had to get my thoughts together for tomorrow's meeting with Captain Wong. The clerk was right, I thought, it was quiet in here.

In the process of dozing off, with subliminal thoughts of listening in on my radio handset, I picked up the sounds of White and his cane. Slowly, they appeared to be closing in on me. I could sense his presence then, feel his weight as he slowly sank onto the lower edge of my cot.

"You're the captain's RTO aren't you?" he said with an almost effeminate tone. Without opening my eyes, I nodded my head.

"McCormick," he said. Great! Two points for him, I thought. My name's on my knapsack and also on my fatigue shirt.

"You feel up to talking?" he asked.

I told him I was tired and I had an important early morning meeting.

"Is it about me?" he inquired, slurring his words. One of the repercussions from shooting yourself in the foot must be paranoia, I mused. I told him no, that it was a private matter with S-2.

"McCormick. McCormick, I'm sorry, what's, what's your first name?" he stuttered in a soft toned manner. I told him it was David.

"David," he said. "Look, David, I don't know what they are thinking about me out in the field and, honestly, I don't give a damn. The Army is fucked up. You understand? This war is fucked up. I don't know if you can appreciate this but I just wanted off line. Do you hear what I'm saying? That's all. I wanted off line. I reached the end of my chain. Going out every day. Guys get'n blown away. The lieutenant fuck'n with you. The sergeant sends you out on LPs. The night ambushes. Always wondering, are you gonna come back? Are you gonna get shot? I mean, last month I pretty near stepped on a mine that would have blown my fuck'n leg off."

There was a lengthy lull in our one-sided conversation. Then, leaning over my body he whispered into my ear, "McCormick." The smell of beer was pungent. "David." I was hoping he was not about to get sick on me. "Dave." I also hoped he wasn't about to kiss me.

"I… wanted… off… line. That's all. I wanted off line. Can you tell me you don't think of this? And if for some God-forsaken fuck'n ass reason you don't think of gett'n off line, does that make you better than me?" There was a long-lasting silence. Then the empty bottle, apparently one of many, fell to the floor as White unceremoniously passed out alongside of me. I reflected for a few moments what to do with him, while waiting for a potential postscript. He was out. Dead to this world. After a moment, rather than picking him up and attempting to carry him back to his spot, I just got up, shifted his body onto my cot, tried to make him comfortable, and moved myself over to the one next to him.

I woke the next morning to the sound of someone informing White he had KP. He didn't seem too pleased. It was about 4:45 and still dark out. I got up thinking what a luxury it was to have slept on a cot with a mattress, to have a roof over my head, and to be without the responsibilities that accompanied me when my right hand is wrapped around a handset. I amused myself for a few moments watching White fumble as he located and then put on his shorts, which he apparently removed during the night. I then headed to the showers, got dressed and went for breakfast. By 7 AM I was standing directly across the street from S-2. I paused there, attempting to work up the stamina to approach my former commander with my special request. The self-assurance and bravado that had accompanied me on this entire trip had waned immensely over the past twelve hours, compliments of one Private White.

Am I any better than him trying to get off line, I thought? Should I even be here right now? The screen door to the building opened. Standing in the center of the doorway and looking in my direction was Captain Wong. Of the many months I spent on line as the captain's RTO and using one hand, I could very easily count the number of times I witnessed Captain Wong smile. This was one of them. A cup of coffee in one hand, a clipboard in the other and wearing a pair of freshly starched fatigues, he strutted down the walkway and across the road. He looked relaxed and at ease with himself, traits I could not attest to when we were in the field.

"Mac, what brings you into town?" placing coffee and clipboard down and shaking my hand with both of his. I was direct and to the point.

"Sir, I'm scared. The new CO. He's not at all like you. I think he's going to get someone killed. I'm really scared. I was just wondering if there was anything that you could do to get me off line?" He told me he wasn't sure he could do anything for me but would see what he could do. He did add one thing, though. He asked me to give the new CO a chance, to give him more time. He also said there was no one in the entire division that was better at their job than I. "You're an asset, Mac, and the Company needs you. It needs you where you are. You're a good communicator and you know your stuff."

By early afternoon I was in the front seat of a jeep that was part of a convoy heading back to our base camp. I returned with a new perspective on things. And if only for the fact I had a 24-hour reprieve from this crazy war, I was feeling pretty good about myself. I was thinking about the last thing White said to me before passing out. Does that make you better than me? Well, I thought, at least I didn't have to shoot myself to get an answer. That was the last time I saw Captain Wong and I never followed up with my request to get off line.

That evening, the officers and the platoon leaders were called into the command bunker for a briefing on recent enemy activity. C Company was recently ambushed in broad daylight by what was believed to have been several platoons of Vietcong. Two men were killed and nearly a half dozen wounded with no enemy body count. Bravo Company was given orders to help track down and engage this enemy force. To date, under the leadership of the new CO, we had minimum encounters with the enemy. Taking on a mission such as this against a considerable strength would be the first true test of the new CO's capabilities and competence.

Early the next morning, our company gathered in formation outside the wire and waited to be airlifted out. Soon after, a dozen or so hueys arrived. Moments later we were airborne. We traveled fast and low, over farms and rice paddies, water buffalos and Mama-sans, keeping a good distance between the unknown dangers that might be lurking between the wood lines and our air-born convoy. As we began our descent in the approximate vicinity of where the enemy was last engaged, the several dozen door gunners opened fire and saturated the landing zone with their M-60 machine guns.

A point man was assigned and, without delay, Bravo Company and its four platoons were on the move. Within a few minutes I received a call from the 1st Platoon's RTO stating they had just stumbled across a bunker that appeared to be empty. It was so well camouflaged, the experienced man walking point had completely passed over it. It was plain to see how members of C Company had walked into it.

Scattered about were the remains of what is left behind after a firefight: empty ammo packs and blood-soiled bandages, hundreds of spent cartridge shells and a soldier's boot and a helmet liner, remnants of torn and cut up pieces of military fatigues, a used cylinder of an M-72 rocket launcher, a dead radio battery along with several empty cigarette packs. The U.S. military, not wanting to assist the enemy in any way, did a fairly good job in policing up for itself after a battle. Whatever was left behind the local villagers quickly scavenged. The fact the battle had taken place only a few days ago and the villagers had yet to rummage through anything that may have been left over was not a good sign.

"What do you think, Mac?" This was the first time the new CO had asked my opinion on anything. Thinking about what Captain Wong had said to me yesterday morning, "You're an asset and the company needs you"; I responded, "The enemy may be gone but they are cruising the neighborhood." I radioed TOC headquarters to tell them of our find. We moved out and continued the hunt. It was a little past 9 AM.

By noon, having been on the move for almost three hours, the CO gave orders for the company to hold up and take a thirty-minute break for lunch. It was exceptionally hot and especially humid for the time of day and there appeared to be little relief in sight. Within minutes of taking our break the unmistakable sound of enemy AK-47 rifle fire was heard in the distance. Moments later we were on the move in the direction of the rifle fire. By 2 PM, with no sound or sign of the enemy, we again halted. We had been on the run without a break for close to an hour, and with the heat the men were worn down.

We came across a small clearing adjacent to the wood line, and we were about to be gifted with some down time. The first, second and fourth platoons were to move to the inside edge of the woods and keep a lookout for the enemy. The third platoon, along with the CO and myself, would take the forward more open area where we could keep watch over the path where we had just come. As I was settling in, TOC called and requested our location. I gave the handset to the captain and walked away to take a leak in the woods. When I returned, sitting by the radio was someone who had been on line for a number of months yet I hadn't really gotten to know. His name was James Roberg. He was sort of an everyday looking type of a guy, fair skinned with thinning light colored hair and a small, neatly trimmed moustache. He had a calm way about him and could have been a teacher or an accountant back stateside. He told me he was from Minnesota, and so I nicknamed him Minnesota.

We talked for a good while. He told me a little about Minnesota. I told him a little about New York. We talked about our birthdays being in July, mine the 5th, his the 14th. He was pleasant, low key and down to earth. At 18, he was a bit younger than most on line. He seemed to harbor no grudge as he told the story of how a recruiting sergeant had talked him into signing up for an extra year in return for a guarantee he would not be given an 11B. (11B was the military classification for infantry foot soldier and, if sent to Vietnam, you were all but assured combat duty.)

"Well," Minnesota said, "here I am, 11B, in infantry and on line. So much for guarantees. I plan on having a little talk with that army recruiter when I return home." For someone who got shafted that badly, his disposition was remarkably composed. Though I felt bad for him, I also admired him for his overall outlook and did not think very much of the military recruiter who deceived him. I had heard stories like this before.

Worn out and wanting to get some rest, I asked Minnesota if he would monitor my radio for a while. I told him there were only two types of calls he might get, one from TOC headquarters, the other from one of our platoons. TOC usually just wanted to know location grids and the captain just gave that to them so he wouldn't have to be concerned about that. I also told him to listen carefully, especially if one of the other platoons was calling as they may be reporting on enemy activity. He seemed comfortable with this and I had confidence in him. I moved away about ten yards, made a pillow out of my backpack, unbuttoned my shirt and lay down at the base of a tree. My M-16 was at my side.

It took me a while to unwind but when I did I was out cold. It was a deep but troubled sleep, as the heat of the day had not let up. It lasted about thirty minutes. As I opened my eyes I saw several of the men sprawled out on the ground in front of me trying to get some rest. Beyond them, with their backs to the captain, were two men sitting guard duty, scrutinizing the path we had been on earlier. Next to them was the third platoon RTO, Ken Sikes, handset to ear, monitoring his radio. Minnesota, being alone as before, was sitting upright with his back leaning against a downed tree that had toppled over in another time. A dozen more men were in a large circle, some were eating and others were playing cards. All were discussing stories of being stateside. The captain, sitting on a log about twenty feet from Minnesota, had my radio and was talking into the handset.

As I became fully awake, I was curious to note we had company. On the horizon, a good distance away, was a helicopter that appeared to be hovering in place. Since it was so far off, I could not determine what kind it was. In addition we seemed to be upwind and I was not able to fully hear the sound of the engine, always a giveaway as to the type. I assumed it to be either a LOCH (Light Observer Carrying Helicopter) or a huey (passenger carrying helicopter). Staring up at it, I wondered if it had anything to do with the captain's communicating on the radio. I got up, went over and squatted down next to Minnesota. "How ya do'n?" I asked.

"Hot," he responded.

"What's with the chopper?" I inquired.

"I don't know, but it did a quick flyby down a ways while you were sleep'n," he said.

"Did you see what kind it is?" I asked.

"No, it was too quick and the tree line covered it," Minnesota responded.

"Is the captain speaking with TOC?" I asked.

"He's talk'n to someone from the first platoon. I don't know what about," he replied.

Except for the faint drone of the helicopter, it was quiet and peaceful. Feeling hungry and wanting to get something to eat, I stood up and began to walk over to my backpack to get some C-rations. Then Minnesota called out, "You were right about TOC."

"What do you mean?" I called back, rather blasé.

"They called and asked for our location," he said. I kept walking towards my backpack trying to remember what type of C-rations I had packed and what I would be eating. "Twice," he added. With my back to Minnesota I froze in place. Twice? That would make it three times inside of thirty minutes. I turned my head towards the captain. He was still on the radio. Behind him, with no change in location, the helicopter remained hovering.

Having spent over six months on line, you develop a sense when something isn't right. Call it intuition if you will, but you somehow get it. I started to get that feeling now. One of the signs of this is a sickening sensation that starts in the pit of your stomach. I knew something wasn't right but I wasn't altogether sure what. One thing I did know was a helicopter pilot's greatest fear is being the target of an enemy rocket-propelled grenade launcher. To see one remain stationary for any period of time is highly unusual. The fact TOC headquarters had in the past gone hours without asking our location and now hit us up three times inside of thirty minutes just did not make sense. Add to it my suspicions of the CO, new to the company, who might not be one hundred percent sure of our grids and locations.

In a near trance-like state, I slowly turned and looked over at the 3rd platoon's radiotelephone operator. His handset was still pinned to his ear. I then looked down at his radio. With a controlled sense of urgency and without looking back, I walked over to his position. The two men sitting guard duty were chatting and oblivious to my presence. Guardedly, I dropped to my knees, reached over and grabbed his radio. The RTO gave me a puzzled glance. Spinning it around I broke away one of the four rocket flares that was strapped to the back of his radio. At the same time I very subtly asked RTO

103

Sikes, "What do you know about that hovering chopper off in the distance?" The RTO, with handset still to his ear, looked up and over my shoulder in a state of perplexity. I didn't even wait for a response. I figured if the worst case scenario was about to happen, I had only a matter of seconds to react. I walked towards the captain. The chopper was in the process of turning in our direction. I was tense and not altogether sure I was doing the right thing. The helicopter had now completed its turn. Slowly, it was heading in towards us. I stood just a few feet from the captain with the rocket flare in my hand.

"Just what do you think you're doing?" the captain asked, interrupting his radio transmission. As I peered over his shoulder I immediately became conscious of the fact this was not a huey or a LOCH. Its distinctive and unmistakable shape was what I suspected and feared, a deadly Cobra gunship. The Cobra's only purpose is to hunt and to kill. The captain, suddenly aware of the panic in my eyes, asked once more, "McCormick! What the…"

"That's a Cobra coming at us, sir," I yelled out interrupting him. "I want permission to fire this flare."

"That's a negative! Are you crazy? You heard the AK-47's. We will not give our position away to the enemy," he said as he lowered the handset and turned around into the direction of the helicopter. The Cobra had picked up speed and was closing in fast.

"Does he have our correct grids (location)?" I asked the captain. Getting no response, I looked up at the Cobra. His nose was down and his tail was up, clearly a sign of attack position. I again asked, "Does he have our correct…"

The firing and impact of the Cobra's first rocket was almost instantaneous. The second, third, and fourth exploded around us immediately after. I went flying backwards and landed center of the two men who were sitting guard duty. The captain was thrown in the opposite direction. The tree under which I was sleeping earlier had been hit and became partially split in two. Miniature balls of fire dripped from the branches and down the base of the trunk. The brightness of the afternoon sun was overshadowed as what appeared to be a hundred thousand bits and pieces of leaves and jungle bush rained down upon us. Dirt and smoke engulfed our campsite. The smell of gunpowder was heavy and permeated throughout. There was a moment of complete silence. Then, the inevitable follow-up. The firing of the iniquitous Cobra mini-guns, capable of placing one round of ammunition into every square foot of an area the size of a football field, brought forth screams and cries from those who were hit. Fortunately for us, there were only two short bursts. The Cobra had finished the first assault and began to turn away to make ready for the next.

Thankfully, on this first attack, I was not hit. I also knew I only had less than thirty seconds before the next strike. The flare I had earlier was nowhere in sight. I jumped up and dove for my radio. It was lying flat with the antenna down. Propping it up I re-connected the antenna. Grabbing the dirt filled handset I made a call I was sure would be my last. "TOC, TOC, this is Charlie Papa, friendlies on the ground, friendlies on the ground, friendlies on the ground. Cobra cease fire, Cobra cease fire." Having basically no cover, I looked up from the ground and observed the Cobra as it was completing its final turn in preparation for another onslaught. In the background, cries for medic could be heard again and again and again. With strained emotion, Ken Sikes, the third platoon RTO stuttered into his handset, "Cobra cease fire, Cobra cease fire, friendlies on the ground, friendlies on the ground. Cobra cease fire, Cobra cease fire, friendlies on the ground, friendlies on the ground."

As I listened to Sikes frantically making those calls I was painfully aware the chances of the Cobra gunship being on the same frequency as ours was slim to none. Throwing my radio to the ground I ripped off one of my own flares. I knew I would not be able to set it off in my prone position. Getting up and partially kneeling, I was now totally exposed and staring directly into the nose of the Cobra gunship as it completed its turn. It was heading directly at us. Ripping off the flare's protective cap, I began to pray out loud, "Dear God, if it's meant to be, make it be quick, please, please, please just make it be quick." As the Cobra was in the process of dropping its nose, I slammed the bottom of the flare, housing the trigger mechanism, down onto my knee once, twice, three times without success. It did not fire.

With the gunship closing in, I was faced with only two options. I could throw away the flare that appeared to be a potential dud and grab a new one, which might take up to five seconds or more. Or I could take a chance by giving this one another try. The Cobra was now in full attack position, the nose down, the tail up. I felt I did not have five seconds. I raised the flare up over my head and with all the might and power and emotion from within, I slammed it down onto the topside of the corner of my radio. SWISH. The flare discharged. It created a trail of red smoke, the international distress signal, as it raced upward and directly in front of the Cobra. Without hesitation, the pilot pulled up and turned away.

Ignoring the burning sensation about my hand and face I grabbed my handset to listen in and try to make some sense of what had just taken place. At the same time, I grabbed another flare and just held on to it.

"Dave, Dave, TOC is on the line and wants the CO," Sikes called out. As the captain approached I suggested he use the 3rd platoon's radio in order for me to take a count of our dead and wounded and call in the necessary medevacs. The 1st, 2nd and 4th platoons had reported no deaths and minor injuries. Apparently we in the 3rd platoon had taken the brunt of the assault. Bill Fabicortore, Bravo Company base camp communications engineer, had monitored the whole incident and later informed me we were not in the grid location we said we were in. Consequently, the pilot of the Cobra, spotting our platoon and thinking us to be the enemy, asked for and received permission from TOC to open fire. For various reasons, Bill and I had not gotten along in the past. A lot of this was my problem, as I would always pick on him for not having to go out on ambush due to a medical condition and being overweight. At this moment, though, he was one hundred percent in my corner and assisted me with the medical evacuations and other necessities.

The captain was sitting on a tree stump next to one of the lieutenants. He had the radio handset in one hand, the map in the other. As the medic ran by me he inquired how long before the medevacs would be arriving. I told him no more than five minutes and asked if any of the men were hurt very seriously. On the move and without stopping he called back, "I can't do much for the one by the tree. What did you call him? Minnesota, he's gone."

In war there are only a very few times when you experience most of the emotions you are capable of feeling all at once. Love, hate, anger, confusion, pain, happiness. For me, this was one of those times. In the brief period I spent with Minnesota, I loved his attitude. I hated the thought he was gone. I was angry at the fact the recruiting sergeant had screwed him over and he should not have been here in the first place. I was totally confused why this had all happened to us. I was experiencing the pain of losing someone, but I was happy for him that he would no longer be a part of all this insanity.

When the last of the medevacs had safely lifted off, orders were given to terminate the remainder of our mission and for Bravo Company to be immediately airlifted out and delivered in its entirety to brigade headquarters in Dau Tieng. Once on the ground in Dau Tieng a convoy of trucks, accompanied by military police, escorted us to the large two-story building that was used to house brigade headquarters. There we offloaded and stood in formation facing the front. The aged French-built structure was an impressive one. There were about a half dozen steps that led up to a large wooden porch with columns all around. In all probability it had at one time housed an owner and caretaker of the Michelin Rubber Plantation, a section of real estate I was quite familiar with and had fought many battles in. Guards stood on either side of the large double door entrance.

After a brief period of time one of the two screen doors opened and out stepped the division head, Colonel Maddox. "Attention!" was called out by one of the guards. The entire company came to attention. He was an older, distinguished looking gentleman with a full head of whitish hair. His facial features made no attempt to suppress the seriousness of what had taken place only hours ago. There he stood, silently, with great deliberation, looking out at our troops. It appeared he was making an effort, if only for an instant, to make eye contact with each and every member of our company. For a moment, he bowed his head. He then, with careful and restrained movements, stepped down from the porch and addressed the members of Bravo Company.

"Gentlemen, at ease," he softly called out. "I am well aware of what happened to you men out in the field today. There's not a whole lot I can say to you at this time about today's occurrence as we are still in the process of studying the facts. You were called in here today so I could meet you face to face. I also want you to know that the pilot who flew the Cobra this afternoon is inside and he is very, very upset and highly distraught over this incident."

The colonel was talking to us in a tone and manner such as a caring grandparent may use when speaking to a grandchild. He continued. "War is bad enough as it is and we can't be having you men feel that things like this will be happening again. We need you to maintain your confidence out there. And that the support that is offered you will be there for you when you need it. We here at division will make every effort in seeing to it that this type of thing will not again happen to you or any other unit working in the field. You, all of you are very fine men. And I mean that. I know the officers of Bravo Company. I've even had the opportunity to meet with some of you men out in the field a few times. Now I also want to say that the pilot, though very shaken up over this, had asked me if it was all right for him to come out and speak to you all. I told him yes. I think that may be a good idea."

The colonel then pointed to one of his aides who hurried inside. A few seconds later, the screen door opened and out walked the warrant officer who had piloted the Cobra. His head was bowed, his hands held tightly together in front. Whispers and, understandably, a few off-color comments, circulated among the troops. The pilot stood there in silence for a moment. Then, with what appeared to be great difficulty, he slowly raised his head. As he looked out into our group he said, "I had asked the colonel if I may speak to you today." Clearly he had difficulty speaking. "And I just wanted to extend my most sincere and deepest apologies to all of you. As the colonel had said, we are here to provide support for you. That is our sole mission. I also wanted to say that I love flying. This has been my life. My career. Yet, after something like this, I don't know if I will ever be able to climb back into that cockpit again. I am terribly sorry." With that said, the pilot again tilted his head down and the colonel took over.

"If any of you have any questions about today's incident perhaps now is the time to ask." There was a short pause. "If not, I understand. It should also be noted that you are being given a two day stand-down right here in Dau Tieng. In addition, I want you to know that my door will be open to anyone who has any questions or anything to say while you are here with us."

Though many, I am sure, had questions to ask, no one spoke up. We stood there at ease and in silence for a good minute. The colonel then thanked us for coming. Once again the order bringing us to attention was called out as the colonel and his entourage, along with the pilot, went back inside. As the order was given to dismiss, the men wasted no time and scattered in all directions. And, if only for a precious number of hours, we did what is done to re-create and sample a taste of normalcy. We ate and drank, showered and slept. Some of the men took comfort by writing letters home, others by sneaking over the wire to the local brothel.

Later that evening I found myself stretched out on a cot in one of the barracks that was assigned to our company. It was a large one-story building that was able to accommodate about sixty of us. I also did something that was very unusual for me. I stayed up the entire night, not because I was doing anything special, not because I was with anyone and immersed in some profound conversation. I stayed up because I did not want this down time to end. I stayed up because only a matter of hours ago and for the umpteenth time, I came within inches of losing my life. It was almost as if I was afraid to go to sleep. Lying there by myself, staring out at my surroundings, I just wanted to enjoy the moment. I did not want the night to end.

By 3 AM most of the cots in the dimly lit room were filled. The few stragglers that were entering did so in a respectable and quiet manner. I watched from a distance as one of our new recruits, who couldn't have been more than eighteen and who obviously had a beer too many, was carried in and placed down on an empty cot by someone I had not seen before. I stared in silence as the stranger began to slowly untie and remove the young soldier's boots. First the left, then the right. He then unbuttoned and removed the soldier's pants, then his shirt. How so very kind and civilized that was, I thought. Then, without warning, I did everything I could do to control laughter as the stranger not so delicately ripped away a poncho liner that was covering someone in the neighboring cot and placed it over his charge. With a soft pat on the young soldier's face, the stranger disappeared off into the darkness.

At the far end of the building, there were two guys sitting up and engaged in a conversation that was barely audible. One was smoking. The other had his hand firmly grasped around the neck of a bottle of Jack Daniels. Across from me and two or three cots over, I could detect the steady cadence underneath a towel that was partially covering one of the guys. Around 5 AM I remembered one of the

109

things I placed in my backpack the day before was a small Instamatic camera. I wanted to take one photo of the Cobra before returning to the field, I thought. I also needed to get some sleep.

The rest of the day brought forth a flow of rumors about the friendly-fire incident. Some seemed far-fetched. None were verifiable. One was the helicopter pilot was to be court-martialed. (That could be.) Another was the pilot committed suicide. (I don't think so.) And still another was the enemy was listening in on our frequency, had set us up by firing their AK-47's and then crept up to our position and exposed themselves to the Cobra as it did a flyby. (That sounded interesting but was really stretching it.) There was another rumor that seemed to snowball as the day progressed. Though this one was without details, it did appear to be conceivable. And that was our captain was relieved of his command and a new replacement was brought in and was being briefed by division.

At the forty-eighth hour as the end had come, the members of Bravo Company, slowly, dutifully and perhaps not in the best of condition fell into formation. The several dozen or so trucks, some containing mail and supplies, were waiting and ready for the return run to our base camp. Diesel fumes besieged the troops as only a short distance outside the wire our escort of a half dozen heavily armed jeeps along with several tanks waited with their engines running. Behind us, on a large flagpole, the colors were being raised. Roll call had begun and one by one as names were called out, seats were taken. Watching the men as they boarded the trucks, and at the same time searching up and down the column of soldiers it became apparent one of the rumors that had been circulating had a ring of truth to it. As I handed my radio to one of the privates, I pulled myself up and climbed aboard one of the very last trucks. On this trip back to the field I would be returning without my captain.

CHANGING OF THE GUARD

July 1969

Dearest David,

Aunt Betty sailed her sunfish from Corn Hill to P-town and back last Friday. For me, that would be like going from here to the moon. Anyway, the next day, some local fisherman caught a shark in the fishnets off North Truro. She is so full of adventure...

We miss you...

Love,

The Mother

PS – Walk on the sidewalk

Although only twenty minutes long, it was a deep and restful sleep and when I awakened I felt comfortably relaxed. It was the type of relaxation you might experience when waking up late in your own bed on a Saturday morning with nothing planned for the day. I had been leaning with my back up against the side of a mud and grass wall that made up one of the many huts in the small village where we had stopped to take a break. As I stretched out and opened my eyes I was astounded to see a dozen or more children surrounding me. Except for the way they were clothed I could very well have been in the Land of Oz. I felt as if I was on exhibit in front of all these youngsters. At first, I didn't know what to make of all this until one of the older ones who was standing in the middle snapped to attention and saluted me. Still baffled by all this attention I just smiled and saluted him back. Then one of the younger children moved in on me, lifted a hand as he pointed a finger at my collar and called out two words in utter fascination, "Number one." Bingo.

111

Earlier, since the morning mission was uneventful and I was somewhat bored, I had taken a pen and, as a joke, drawn in four small stars on my collar prior to falling asleep. The children, perhaps having seen a real-life general before, though not necessarily on our side, thought I was the real thing. Looking around at my little audience I took pleasure, if only for the moment, and basked in my newfound celebrity. But I also knew I had to set them straight. Unbuttoning and removing my shirt I took the same pen and drew a line through the stars and at the same time shook my head left to right repeating the words "no number one, no general." The very last thing I wanted any of the villagers to think was I was an officer, especially such a high ranking one. Word travels fast in these small villages and the enemy is always on the lookout for a target. An officer, of course, is a prime target. Particularly if you are six foot six as was our new CO.

He had only been with our company about three weeks and was assigned to us just after the friendly-fire incident. His name was Captain Henry P. Bergson. He was an armor officer who had recently completed a tour of duty in Germany. Back home, his wife, Jackie, a music major, was living on the campus of the University of New Hampshire. At the age of twenty-five they had no children. As officers stood, and besides being tall, he was an affable fellow with a pleasant smile and a kind disposition. Observing him during his first few days he seemed to be what we referred to as someone who "had his stuff together." Putting all this aside, he was also someone who was being watched and carefully scrutinized by a good number of the men, particularly by the men of the 3rd platoon who only weeks ago took the brunt of the friendly-fire incident. By taking over the reins of our company, Captain Hank Bergson, through no fault of his own, inherited excess baggage. The earlier friendly-fire incident still weighed heavily on the minds of many of the men who escaped without injury on that ill-fated day. Whether he knew it or not, this was one captain who had to prove himself to the members of Bravo Company.

"So has he screwed up yet?" came the comment from Ken Sikes as he sauntered by my little sideshow.

"Ken, I thought for sure I had him yesterday on the daylight ambush," I answered, then continued, "Clearly he was not in the grids (location) he had me call into TOC headquarters. I checked, checked twice, he was off. I even asked the F.O. (artillery forward observer) and the F.O. agreed with me, the captain's grids did not match his."

"Did you call him on it?" Ken inquired, with curiosity piqued.

"Well, kind of," I responded.

"What do you mean, kind of?" Sikes retorted, a little miffed I wasn't more confrontational with the new captain, then added, "I would have waved the map in his face and said hey, what gives here, we don't need another friendly-fire incident."

"Well, I didn't quite get that far with him and since he is new I wanted to be a bit more diplomatic and give him the benefit of a doubt," I responded, "so I borrowed the F.O.s map and approached the CO with it."

"Yeah," Sikes commented, "so what was Bergson's excuse?"

Actually he didn't have an excuse. This is because he didn't need one. The captain was in the correct grid locations. New maps, consisting of satellite photographs, were recently issued and due to a shortage and limited quantities, company commanders were first to receive them. They were detailed in every aspect and could even pinpoint a fallen tree limb.

"So, he didn't goof up?" Ken questioned.

"This time, no," I responded, "but I am sure we can get him on something else."

Having been out on line with the new CO for this short period of time, it was difficult to determine what, if any, his weaknesses were. For sure, reading the map and knowing his location was not one of them. A major plus. This, however, did not deter many of the members of Bravo Company from keeping an eye on his every move. But proving himself to the company as the new commander was the very least of his problems.

Back in the States, President Nixon was getting a lot of pressure to wind down this war and bring it to a peaceful and honorable end. All sorts of rumors were flying, the best of which was our unit, the 25th Infantry Division, was to be pulled out and sent to home base in Hawaii. Though we never did pull out, what did change and go into effect immediately was a modification and title adjustment to our daily missions. From here on in operations were no longer referred to as "Search and Destroy." The United States government wanted to show the American public it was responsive to their protests, phone calls and letter writing. The new buzzword to be used on all operations was now "Search and *Clear,*" accordingly giving our missions a more humanitarian façade.

Guidelines filtered down from top brass. The burning of huts of known or suspected enemy sympathizers, a common practice of many companies, was to cease immediately. In the past, Captain Wong always frowned on this type of strategy, believing it was better PR to leave the villages as they were, especially when they housed children and elderly. More notably, costly and high profile air strikes, both offensive and defensive, were to be sharply curtailed by all units. Permission for supportive air strikes would now have to be cleared by "higher-ups" and even then to be used only as a last resort.

There was little doubt in anyone's mind these modifications were a direct result of all the stateside protesting. The ordinary citizen back home was demanding an end to this war and a stop to the daily killings that overflowed into their living rooms on the six o'clock news. The downside and disturbing irony here was, by restricting our defensive air strikes, you were effectively taking away our foremost tactical advantage. This was indeed good for the enemy. It was not at all good for us. For South Vietnam a major turning point had now taken place in their fight for independence.

A few weeks later we were sent into Haunigh, an area just a little southwest of Bao Tri, to track down some snipers who were taking a heavy toll on our daily patrols. By mid morning on our second day out I received calls from the first and second platoons claiming enemy sightings. We tracked and pursued. Over the next few hours there were several additional sightings but they always seemed to stay one step ahead of us.

By noontime we came across a small colonial manor house. Before Vietnam I knew very little about French architecture. As we approached we could see it had withstood many a firefight. Most of the windows had been knocked out and the front entranceway blown off. It had a small stone porch that ran the width of the structure. We decided to stop here for a break. The plan was to set up a command center for the purpose of sending out patrols in different directions in hopes of cornering the enemy. This sounded fine to me, especially since I knew that being the command RTO I would not be part of these patrols.

As we approached, I couldn't help but admire the charm and character of this attractive home. In a curious way, it was almost like a magnet drawing us in. The windows were blown out. From our distance it looked to be dark inside. The walls were pockmarked with bullet holes. Unbeknown to us, lying in wait inside this structure were several enemy snipers who had been harassing our troops over the past several weeks.

Captain Bergson ordered several men to scout out the side and back of the house, while he and I, along with two other members of the third platoon, walked up to the front entrance. It was all quiet and peaceful. As the captain and I stepped onto the front porch, several hand grenades were tossed outside and exploded. At the same time we began to receive sniper fire from various points.

Except for the four of us, the majority of the 3rd platoon had been walking behind, perhaps no more than fifty feet. Everyone hit the ground. Since we were directly on the porch and hugging the walls, no one from the 3rd platoon wanted to open fire for fear of hitting us. Having a new captain get shot by his own men would not make the best of headlines. We were not about to make a run for it as we were concerned about being shot at from within. It was then the captain said to me, "Dave, any suggestions on how to get out of this mess will be highly entertained." I responded by using some newly developed vocabulary and said, "I think this is a shitty situation we don't need to be in right now. I would call in a Cobra gunship. The sound alone should scare the crap out of anyone inside. Then I'd have him scout and spray the area while we pull back and regroup." A brief discussion existed between the two of us about whether a Cobra was overkill and an even shorter talk about the newly instituted policy from higher-ups to cut back on air power. Then another grenade went off. "Do it," the captain ordered.

Not only did Captain Bergson allow me to call in the gunship, he allowed me to direct the fire, something I was good at and confident about, yet hadn't done since under the leadership of Captain Wong. I liked the fact he not only asked my advice, he actually took it. But more importantly than that and even after taking into account the directives that had come down from Washington to avoid unnecessary use of air-strikes, he authorized the strike. Whether he knew it or not, this new CO had just laid some new groundwork. By allowing the use of air-power he took a stretch and a stand. He bucked the system. If Washington sent down orders, fine, he would follow them, but not at the cost or safety of his men. He also proved to the members of Bravo Company he was his own man. He was the captain and he was in charge.

Over the next few missions I became very much in tune with the style of our new leader, and we seemed to work together in harmony: I, drawing on my past experiences with enemy encounters; he, sharing his plans of action prior to our daily missions. We were truly in sync with one another. If there were any lingering doubts from any of the members of Bravo Company about this captain's ability to lead, they were not voiced to me. Having been on the battlefield for less than thirty days' time, Captain Henry P. Bergson crossed that invisible line that exists between all commanders and the men they lead. He had earned their trust.

It appeared Captain Bergson also wanted to minimize the blood shed on both sides. Under his leadership our daily operations appeared to take on a new air of excitement. Strange as it may sound, I, along with a good many of the others, actually looked forward to going out on some of the missions. The focus now it seemed was not so much on an ambush or an attack, but more so on the hunt. We worked closely with special members of the South Vietnamese Army task force. Instead of an enemy kill, all efforts it seemed were now centered on an enemy capture. The new philosophy that was being set in motion was an enemy captured alive is worth considerably more than several dead. The prized body count that certain members of Congress and the administration were so focused on obtaining would have to take a back seat. One thing, however, did not change. If it came down to an encounter with the enemy where the circumstances and likelihood of a capture were questionable, the enemy would be engaged. This was understood by all the men.

Getting beyond the first thirty days with our new CO I was, for the first time since I could remember, experiencing a positive and upbeat attitude. I even allowed myself to think about the idea of actually surviving this war and the possibility of going home in one piece. I had yet to take a leave, which I was entitled to and felt perhaps now was the time to start planning for this. These good feelings I had, along with the relationship between Captain Bergson and me, seemed to give me license to feel I could do no wrong. The working relationship I had going with Captain Bergson was not just a team effort, it was a bond of trust. At the time the company consisted of approximately ninety men and was well prepared to handle almost any situation. If there was such a thing as a super-bowl of battles or confrontations, the members of Bravo Company were ready, willing and sufficiently able to handle it. We were a team working in unison. With the smooth way things were going, certainly the very last thing on my mind was during the next enemy encounter, I and I alone would be the one to drop the ball.

(The time was 10:55 PM. Slowly I switched the safety on my weapon from off to automatic. My finger poised on the trigger. A round was in the chamber. Clearly I had the enemy in my sights. They were approximately 100 feet in front and walking parallel to me in single file formation. Their pace was slow, but steady. At first I spotted only three. Now I could see six and they were still coming. At twelve I stopped counting. Because of my position and location and due to the fact I was up and on guard duty, I was the first to sight them. Without warning they were now directly in front of me. If my focus remained stable and I minimized my spray in the field of fire I could easily take out half of them, and very likely more. All I had to do was squeeze the trigger. I delayed for a moment to see how many more were behind. Twelve seemed to be it. It was now up to me to make the move.)

As it was, the day started out somewhat ominous. Large thick clouds along with the continuous sound of thunder threatened and followed our company all morning long. By late afternoon the monsoon that was building would hold back no longer. Almost as if in retaliation against all wars, the heavens opened up with a vengeance. It was not just a downpour, but more like a mass of water that dropped down upon us. Just prior to the deluge Captain Bergson took note of a small group of huts standing a short distance away. They were situated on an embankment that overlooked the rice paddy we were patrolling through. Figuring a battle or firefight in this type of weather was a lose lose situation, he opted to take refuge and give the men a break along with dry shelter for the evening.

The captain chose to set up our command post in the centermost hut, one that appeared to be built out a bit forward of the others. Ours was the smaller of the shelters and besides Jenkins, a seasoned rifleman, and Fernando, a new recruit, it was just the captain and I. The intensity of the storm remained steady but at least, thankfully, we were out of it. I proceeded to do a radio check making sure all platoons were set up and prepared for the nightfall. Had it not been for the storm our location would have given us a clear, unobstructed view of the rice paddy we had been patrolling through along with the various paths and walkways that divide it. The blend of the storm along with the hour allowed darkness to filter in early. With this combination, our field of vision was restricted to no more than three to six feet. It was approximately 6 PM.

I called our location into TOC headquarters, informing them we were set for ambush and would be here for the night. A familiar voice and one that comforted me was on the return call transmitted by Pete Arnone, who, after being wounded, was now assisting and monitoring battalion radio. My radio checks went well with one exception. The 1st platoon was not responding. They were at the tail end of our patrol and consequently would have been the last to take up their positions. The most recent communication I had with them was at 5:30, about fifteen minutes prior to the storm hitting. Somewhat anxiously I repeated my call. Again no contact. I then called the 3rd platoon and asked if they had a visual of any of the members of the 1st platoon. The response was negative. My concerns for their whereabouts escalated.

The captain suggested the possibility of a dead battery. "Not likely," I responded. "We've only been out twenty-four hours and with minimum transmissions. They can go forty-eight to seventy-two hours. Besides I know they're carrying a spare. If the battery was dead, they would have changed it by now." I continued calling. After a period of time Captain Bergson ordered a runner to be sent from the 3rd platoon to check out the situation. Shortly after, RTO Ken Sikes radioed in that contact was indeed made with the 1st platoon and, with one exception, all was well. Apparently their RTO was not fast enough to wrap his handset with plastic before the rains hit and it had shorted out. Consequently, until it dried, we would be without communication with the members of the 1st platoon. Effectively, this would delay any early warning we might have with any approaching enemy. This was not a good sign. The time was 7:20 PM.

After finishing our meals of C-rations, Jenkins, Fernando and I worked out the night watches. As in the past Captain Bergson offered to take one of the watches. I would take the first three-hour shift. It seemed simple enough as visibility had not improved one bit. By 9 PM the captain, along with the others were stretched out on the cool damp dirt floor. Despite these conditions they seemed to be resting comfortably and we've been in worse situations, I thought. At 10 PM I did my routine radio check.

With the rains falling and visibility still at an all time minimum, there were no reported sightings of enemy movement. Additionally, and more reassuring was the fact no one on guard had fallen asleep. I even made an extra effort to make contact with the 1st platoon. After a few tries, however, it seemed obvious their radio had yet to recover. Deciding to make one final attempt I whispered into the microphone, "Foxtrot Papa (1st platoon) this is Charlie Papa, if you read me press your transmit button once." Straight away the faint but distinctive sound of the airway breaking could be heard through my handset. Excitedly, I radioed back, "Foxtrot Papa, I roger that." Through a series of tests we put in place a simple warning code. They were to click once to signify all was well during a radio check, three times if they spotted movement. Communication, minute as it was, had been reestablished with the 1st platoon. It was now 10:35 PM.

At 10:50 PM and without the slightest warning the rains came to an abrupt halt. It was eerily quiet with the only sounds being the irregular drippings from the rooftop above. The drip, drip, drip sounds were almost hypnotic. Visibility had not improved. The fog bonding with the mist seemed like one big sheet and just hung out there. For all I knew, someone could be standing less than three feet in front of me. It could be Vietcong or NVA. It could be one of our men from a neighboring hut searching around to relieve himself. It could be Bozo the clown. There was just no way of telling. One thing I did know: it was getting close to the end of my watch and I needed to wake Jenkins. I also needed to make a resting spot for myself for the evening. Having lowered the handset from my ear and listening to the dripping sounds, I failed to hear the click, click, click.

Gathering my knapsack I reached in and grabbed my poncho liner. It was still damp from the rains. I was annoyed with myself for not thinking to pull it out and open it earlier to dry. Once more the sounds, click, click, click echoed faintly through my receiver. Again I did not hear it. As I quietly pulled my liner from my pack I began to notice the fog was slowly lifting out front. Visibility was finally returning, first a few feet at a time, then much greater distances. For the first time since nightfall I was able to see the bottom part of one of the paths that lay out front. I watched, first in amazement as the haze continued to lift, then in absolute alarm as what I saw appeared to be the legs of several mist covered torsos walking along the rice paddy directly out in front of me.

Almost as if I was on auto-pilot I reached down to my side, placed my hand firmly around the stare-light (night-vision) scope, flipped on the tiny switch, held it to my eye and waited an excruciating twenty seconds for it to warm up. The fog had now all but disappeared and, along with the illumination from the scope's internal iris, I could plainly see three men walking out in front in a straight line. The soft high-pitched whine of the scope's working mechanism along with my movements stirred awake the sleeping captain. After placing the scope down I lifted my weapon. My sights were trained dead center and on the number two man of the group. Then, from the shadows of darkness, their numbers increased. Captain Bergson, lying on his back and not fully aware of the events unfolding, whispered out to me, "Anything going on out there?" My body was stone rigid, sweat was dripping down from my forehead. Tensely and in a hushed manner I responded, "Got twelve in my sights."

Jenkins, already awake, sitting up and looking out whispered, "What's you gonna do?" The parade of men continued by me until my sights were no longer focused on the middle, but now more towards the end and at their backs. They were more than halfway past me when the captain sat up. Yet, my finger, wrapped tightly around the trigger, would not budge. The captain, now fully awake, called out, "What the hell are you doing? You're letting them get away. Why didn't you shoot?" The last of the group had disappeared off and into the darkness almost as quickly as when they first appeared in front of me. And I had not fired a shot.

The next morning Captain Bergson probed me. He didn't really ask what happened last night as much as he asked what happened to me last night. He inquired how I could let a dozen enemy slip by me without firing a shot. He inquired as to what was going through my head. He also did one other thing that surprised me. He did not push the issue. He gave me space. He let it drop. What I had done or failed to do was a serious matter and not to be taken lightly. If Bergson had a mind to, he could have filed charges against me. But that was not his style. Maybe that one day a few weeks back, on the front porch of the small colonial manor house when I aggressively took charge of the Cobra gunship, was now my saving grace. I don't know. I just know I was grateful he didn't follow up as to why I failed to fire. I was thankful he let me off the hook in return for a minimal explanation. I was also thankful I didn't have to reveal the truth about what actually happened to me last night and what, in fact, had been going on in my head. It took me a while myself to figure it all out, and when I did, it was all really quite simple. The truth of the matter is on that late afternoon on that twenty-second day of June not much more than thirty days back, the war, as I had known it, had ended for me.

The friendly-fire incident, which had wounded so many and snuffed out the life of James Roberg, was still fresh in my mind, but in a very strange way. The intensity of that afternoon's experience is one I will truly never be able to put into words. Yet in these past thirty days my focus and thoughts were not centered on the death of Roberg as much as they were on the pilot who had opened fire on us. For whatever reason, I just couldn't get him out of my mind. On the pilot's second attempt, when he was bearing down and coming straight at me, he was equipped with a massive arsenal of weaponry. I, on the other hand, could only use a smoke flare to fend him off. To an extent it was somewhat reminiscent of a David and Goliath occurrence. And although I was David, he clearly was not Goliath. I did not want to harm him. I just wanted to make him go away. I survived all these many months without once being responsible for a friendly-fire incident. Now, ever since that day, all I could think of was what would it be like to be responsible for one. I wondered what were his thoughts and how did he feel when he learned he had mistakenly opened fire on his own soldiers? How do you live with yourself after such a horrific incident? And once something like this has happened to you, is there any way not to think about it and file it away in your past without going mad?

When the rains stopped and the fog was lifting and I first spotted the three men out front, there was very little doubt in my mind they were Vietcong or NVA. There was also little doubt they had to be engaged. But as the mist cleared revealing a dozen or so men walking in single file formation very much like our own people travel every day, I thought for a moment about how they could have gotten by the 1st platoon without their warning me with the three clicks. Then, for one brief second, with my sights firmly planted on the center man I thought about the Cobra pilot. About friendly-fire. About the fact I did not verbally hear from the 1st platoon all evening. Then I wondered if there was the slightest possibility any of the men walking in front were members of the 1st platoon looking for whatever reason to relocate and without the benefit of radio communication. At that particular moment, all I could think of was that afternoon on the twenty-second day of June. With a percentage of doubt in my mind, no matter how infinitesimal, I could not find it in me to squeeze the trigger. I let them pass.

MY FRIEND DAVE

August 1969

Dearest David,

Well as much as your father hates to fly he took a plane to Mexico today to finalize the divorce.
Holding your birthday gifts for when you return home...

Love,

The Mother

PS – Walk on the sidewalk

It wasn't the look on his face, or the body language or even the needed signature that told him. It was the silence. Mr. Thomas, Sr., had known the postman with the certified letter for a good number of years. The Armed Forces had a policy of making a personal visit to the home before the letter is delivered. For whatever reason, that official visit did not happen on this rainy summer morning in 1969.

Removing his glasses and closing the front door he slowly made his way down the short hallway, then up the stairs of the modest two story Connecticut home, all the while making a mindful effort to keep his emotions in check. Entering the room, he stared down for a second at the neatly made empty bed. He then took an unhurried glance about the area that belonged to his son who was so very far away from home. He reflected for a while before opening the letter.

"Dear Mr. and Mrs. Thomas: On behalf of the President of the United States and the Department of the Army, it is our sad duty to inform you of the death of your son, David Thomas, in the line of duty in the Republic of Vietnam." It was a while before Mr. Thomas finished reading the remainder of the letter. When he did so he decided not to tell his wife who was asleep in the bedroom across the hall.

123

Early in my tour of duty and not too eager to make new friends there developed a relationship between Dave Thomas, the new artillery specialist, and me. Dave was a good-looking Italian, stood about six feet tall and was from Danbury, Connecticut. At first, he seemed to be on the shy side and even displayed a touch of innocence, which was refreshing. It was also surprising. Though new to us, he was not new in country, and in the jungles of Vietnam things like shyness and innocence usually disappear after your first battle. He was assigned to our company and was there for us when situations called for the use of heavy artillery support.

During a firefight, if we found ourselves to be up against a large enemy force, or if we were being attacked from more than one direction, the captain could make a request for additional firepower. Enter Dave Thomas as he or an artillery officer would in turn call in the targeted position, send in a practice sulfur round or two in order to make sure his calculations were correct, then open up with a barrage of 105 howitzer shells (or larger) on the hopefully retreating enemy. Since Dave had to be within listening distance of the captain at all times and I was the captain's RTO, a sort of 'forced' relationship existed between the two of us.

In the beginning, there were two reasons why I did not like Dave. Reason number one, he was new and, therefore, his experience was questionable. In his line of work, one wrong call could easily wipe out a good number of our young men. Friendly-fire was not an uncommon occurrence, especially with the big guns Dave was responsible for. Reason number two, he didn't laugh at any of my jokes. And I was funny. The first few firefights where artillery was called for had tested Dave's talents and abilities for speed and accuracy. If you were to ask me if he truly hit his target, I would be at a loss to say. What I do remember is none of the artillery rounds he called in hit any of us. In my book, with the length of time I had been on line, that in itself was a passing grade.

As the number of missions increased, so did the intensity of our firefights. For sure there would be days at a time without sight or sign of the enemy. Then there would be days when, without the slightest warning, you would have multiple firefights and be up against what appeared to be a large and overwhelming force with countless enemy soldiers firing on you from all directions. It was here Dave's knowledge and skills were put to the true test.

When under fire and having the responsibility and liability of calling in multiple rounds of heavy artillery, and accurately at that, the stress often can be enormous. Yet, at all times, Dave's response and demeanor would be consistent. Always calm. Always focused. More importantly, he was not once responsible for a friendly-fire incident. During times of minor enemy contact when the use of his artillery skills were not called into play, Dave unfailingly would take up an infantry position. He would in effect fight side-by-side with our company. In a time and place where friends around you would very often be wiped out in an instant, Dave offered me a comfort and newfound sense of security simply by his presence.

To be sure, Dave Thomas was not one without flaws. One of the things I found amusing about him was whenever we did get into a firefight, he seemed to take it personally. Dave had a strong yet low-key disposition. When he got upset at something he managed to control his tone and at times it seemed he was holding back on his true feelings. Eventually he accepted and even welcomed my jokes. He would even go so far as to allow me to poke a little fun at his Italian heritage. As time moved along we became very close, a sort of a team. But being shot at by the enemy is where he drew the line. I would try to rationalize with him by explaining when an enemy soldier shoots at us, he is only doing his job, therefore we should not take it personally. Forget it. That wouldn't fly with him.

On this unbearably hot August day, while returning from a mission, we were marching down the center of a wide-open path that was leading back to our base camp. The outer edges were lined with small bushes and wild shrubbery. It was so very reminiscent of the many walks I enjoyed in my youth on Cape Cod while exploring the sand dunes on Corn Hill in the town of Truro. I told Dave about the wonderful clay mines that existed in the back part of the dunes and the small carnivals we created and celebrated for no reason on top of the hill. I confessed to him I experienced my very first kiss on the hill and it was with my cousin Marianne.

"You kissed your cousin?" Dave exclaimed.

"Well, kind of. I mean it was at the carnival and she had this kissing booth."

"Don't tell me, Dave, your cousin charged you, right?" Dave chimed in.

"Well yes, I had to pay her a dollar," I said somewhat sheepishly, then added, "I always wondered if she would have let me kiss her if I didn't have the money." To which Dave retorted, "I'm surprised your cousin Marianne didn't charge you five dollars!"

Continuing on, it soon became obvious the path we were traveling had been used before. Unfortunately, the footprints imbedded in the sand were not those of the familiar military issue combat boots, but instead those of sandals worn by the enemy. Taking this into account the captain ordered me to place all platoons on high alert. At the completion of my last transmission an explosion could be heard forward of the first platoon. It was then we were hit with a volley of enemy mortars. There was absolutely no cover to be found anywhere so we just dove for the ground. Apparently Dave and I were aiming for the same piece of real estate as we landed almost on top of each other.

Dave called out "This is bullshit, man! When we get back to the base camp you and I are gonna build ourselves a bunker. A Goddamn bulletproof, bomb proof, gook proof bunker." The mortars kept falling. I told him he was dreaming and said bunkers like that are for officers and it's not that simple to do. In addition, I added, materials are in short supply and I reminded him he was only attached to and not officially assigned to our company.

"Bullshit, McCormick," he said. I loved his crassness. "You of all people are the king of procurement. If you can't get it, it doesn't exist." Then one of the mortars exploded no more than ten feet from us sending sounds of bells and chimes and parts of Beethoven's fifth ringing in my eardrums.

Thinking it was all over and cashing in on Dave's dream, I played along. "It would have to be steel reinforced," I shouted. Dave, having survived the near miss yelled back, "Absolutely!"

"And the walls, the walls would have to be double width, like the command center," I added attempting to focus on anything other than the sheer terror I was experiencing.

"I can get empty artillery casings and we'll fill them with sand," Dave screamed out, possibly thinking about where the next mortar round may land.

"Electricity, I would want electricity, otherwise, no bunker," I called out with a quiver in my voice and thinking the center of my back had an 'X' on it and could very well be ground zero for the next incoming round.

"Peck," (a nickname he gave me) "I can get you that. Don't ask from where, but I can get you that," Dave responded, an octave or two above his normal voice. Then added, "We could have lights, and a fan."

With my face buried in the sand and my fingernails dug into a helmet very much secured to my head, it seemed as if an eternity before the last of the shells dropped. When it was over, miraculously no one was hit. The captain debated for a moment about the merits of searching out and tracking down the location of the incoming rounds that would lead us to the enemy. With situations like this, past experience had shown it would be like uncovering a needle in the haystack. During an incoming mortar attack while stretched out on the ground without cover and your focal point being self-preservation, the last thought on your mind is the direction of fire. With the enemy, it's more often than not a hit-and-run situation. We got up, dusted ourselves off, cursed them out and continued on.

That evening back at base camp I took a walk over to the artillery compound in search of Dave. I caught him with a face full of shaving cream. "You serious about building our own bunker?" I asked. He turned to me and asked, "Now what do you suppose I should do if we had incoming (mortars) this very moment?" I looked down and saw his helmet was filled with water. There was a long moment of silence. Dave continued his shave. Speaking softly, and concerned I might be overheard I commented, "I understand we have a truckload of replacement troops coming in tomorrow."

"Hey, you're the sergeant," Dave added with a smirk on his face. The mere idea of having our own private bunker started to take on a life of its own. "I could meet the convoy at the gate, grab a few of the new recruits and have the walls up before Top even starts looking for their paperwork," I added.

"And where do you propose we should build this thing?" Dave inquired almost as though the entire idea to build a bunker was mine.

"I've got the spot already picked. It will be directly across from the captain's bunker," I added excitedly.

By noon the following day Dave and I were standing beside four fresh-faced, wide-eyed shirtless young recruits. They sweated away as they scooped dirt, filled sandbags and lay the groundwork towards construction of a bunker that would be capable of taking a direct hit from anything the enemy had in its arsenal. The walls were over one foot thick. The ceiling was made from a single section of corrugated metal. The roof was made up of reinforced steel. It consisted of several segments of track plates that were commonly used to maintain traction on mud soaked roads during monsoon season. How Dave got hold of this is beyond me.

By 2 PM most everything was completed except the small wooden front door when a private approached and said Top wanted to see me. This jig is up, I thought. He never calls for me. Top is gonna nail me for unauthorized use of military personnel. As Top was the highest-ranking non-commissioned officer in the company, I knew I had to come clean with him. I used these new recruits for my own personal benefit. There was no getting around this. Lying to him would only jeopardize my stripes, so that was out of the question. That was until I saw the look on his face.

"McCormick! Just what the hell do you think you are doing?" Top bellowed. I saw he had the new recruits' paperwork in his hand. Top and I were total opposites. He was a career soldier, I was anything but. He was what we refer to as a lifer, someone who eats, sleeps, dreams and lives for the Army. There are only two books in his world, one is the Bible and the other is *the book*. *The book* is what Top goes by. By Top's standards anything else was non-existent.

"Soldier, you have one minute to give me an explanation for corralling up these young men without permission." I couldn't help myself. I had just gotten my stripes and promoted to sergeant only a few weeks ago and I didn't want to lose them. So I did what anyone else would do when caught in a situation such as this. I told him what a career person would want to hear… I lied.

"Top, Sergeant sir, I had this fine bunker built specially for you," I yelled out.

"What the hell are you talking about, soldier? I can't leave the captain's side. We have our own bunker right here and I like it and you aren't moving me, you understand, soldier?" Top snapped.

"Yes, Top," I said rather innocently.

"And get those new soldiers over to Charlie Company before someone's ass gets kicked!" he added.

"Will do, Top," I shouted back in a very respectful manner as I turned to walk away. I was halfway out of the command center's bunker when Top shouted out, "You should think about using that bunker for yourself!"

Dave and I completed the bunker on our own and by week's end the finishing touches, such as an electrical line, stolen from nearby headquarters, and a land-line (telephone), also compliments of the unknowing HQ compound, were installed. It was our home away from home. We had a radio, a small fan and a single hanging electric light bulb. For the first time in nearly a year, there existed a little privacy, a place to escape when not out on a mission, a place to sleep without being concerned about running for cover during sporadic enemy mortar fire. The only problem was, more often than not, Dave and I would be out on assignments. During a week's time, it seemed, five or six out of seven days we were out in the field on overnights conducting sweeps or ambush missions. But at the end of an operation and upon returning to the compound, to us, it was the closest thing to a real life Shangri-la.

I truly enjoyed being around Dave. Hopefully, the feelings were reciprocal. But more than that, and without ever discussing it, while out in the field, unfailingly, we kept an eye out for one another. It was just something that was understood. Free of all the fanfare, we watched each other's backs. Needless to say, a run-in with the enemy, from a sniper attack to a full-blown battle, can be tense. With lives at stake, your attention span is stretched beyond limits you never thought possible. Yet if the situation called for artillery I would do my best to lend an extra ear and listen to Dave as he radioed in grid locations. I felt I was always there for him. And on one night, during the early evening hours in the month of June, he was there for me.

This was the night when an ambush we set in place went horribly wrong and, in fact, completely backfired on us. It was also the very first time I witnessed the enemy using women and young children as a buffer in the belief we would not return fire. Unfortunately, the way events unfolded, the enemy miscalculated. In fact, we did fire back. On women, and on children. This was a decision that was made during the heat of battle, a decision made even after my passionate protests.

We arrived at our chosen ambush site on this particular evening a bit earlier than expected. The sun had a few more minutes before disappearing on us. Ordinarily this would have been an ideal time to set up. However, on this occasion we were not alone, and with little light remaining we were being watched. Our company had settled in on a section of dried up rice paddy in the center of a large open area in expectation of ambushing the enemy on one of the paths that ran the length of the field. It was a nice night, warm and dry, and, after the sun had completely set, the stars above offered us better than fifty percent visibility.

The enemy was reportedly making nightly visits to the area villages to procure supplies. Our positioning would have been fine had they walked this particular path. But there were several other paths we, for whatever reason, chose not to or did not have the manpower to cover. One was on our left flank and ran perpendicular directly in front of three small village huts. Earlier, before darkness set in, we observed several women along with an elderly man tending to a half dozen children out front. From this vantage point, should the enemy choose to come up from behind the village, our unit would be wide open and completely unprotected. As chance would have it, this was the path the enemy decided to use this evening. But most disturbing of all was the fact the counter-ambush they set up to fire at us was from the center of the three huts, the one housing some of the women and all of the children.

It was a little before 9 PM and I had just finished a brief watch. I requested and received permission to move about 200 feet down in an area near the front of the three huts. Earlier, I noticed an old dead tree that had partially fallen. I figured it to be a safe and secure haven for me to get some rest. Within thirty feet of the tree were two of our riflemen, one sitting up on guard with a radio, the other lying on his back attempting to get some rest. Although logistically I was close to our unit, I was not on the same path as everyone else. Instead, I was at the tail end and sitting about fifteen to twenty feet in, alongside the main path that faced the village.

By 9:30 I finished stretching out my poncho liner and was in the process of getting set up for the evening. My weapon on this mission was an M-79 grenade launcher. It made more noise than damage but had the psychological effect of putting the fear of God into anyone within target range. The downside of this weapon was you could only fire one round at a time before you had to reload. Since I was at the tail end of the company and had no one on my left, I pulled out several rounds of ammunition, placed them within arm's reach, and loaded one round into the chamber. As a precautionary measure I pointed the nozzle of the weapon to my left. By so doing, should I be awakened in the dead of night, this would hopefully indicate to me I had friendlies on my right. I took one last look around in order to acclimate myself to the new surroundings. I'm set, I thought to myself. Except for one thing. There were three visitors I just witnessed entering the far right hut.

It was obvious the rifleman on my right witnessed the same as he looked in my direction and displayed three fingers to me. He then awakened the one resting next to him, grabbed the radio and alerted the rest of the company. Within a matter of moments, word went up and down the line we had enemy movement in the small village. Soon after the same three men left the first hut and relocated into the middle one, the hut housing some of the women and all of the children. For me, this was a major dilemma, one for which I was not trained or prepared to handle. It was also the first time in a long while I was away from a radio and did not have the captain at my side.

From the vantage point of the enemy looking out from the center hut, our unit must have appeared to look like ducks in a row. The position our company now found itself in was a particularly precarious one. Besides myself, the rifleman to my right was the only one who could safely open fire without hitting any of our own men. As with all situations involving engagement with the enemy, you are faced with making hard decisions with imperfect information. Often, prior to opening fire, there are numerous questions and even more guesswork. Rarely is there a lot of time. Did the enemy see us? Has our element of surprise been compromised? Are these people spotters for a nearby enemy mortar platoon? Are they themselves armed? Are they merely innocent rice paddy farmers returning late from the fields?

In this particular situation at least some of our questions were answered when suddenly a woman made a run to safety from the center hut. Clinging to her body with arms stretched around her neck was a small child. Being tugged immediately behind were two slightly older children. Unfortunately, her efforts to leave were in vain as she was grabbed from behind and yanked back in by two of the three that had entered. An instant later and from inside the center hut, the enemy opened fire.

(At age eight, while in the third grade, I had gotten into a shoving match with a few of the other children inside a large walk-in coat room at Public School number 16 in Yonkers. Nothing so very unusual for kids our age except it escalated a bit and I found myself throwing a few punches. Accidentally, one of the kids I hit was a girl. Later that day Mrs. MacNamara, the school principal, gave me a note to take home regarding the incident. After I arrived home I remembered being scolded by my mother. She lectured me and told me she wasn't so concerned about my getting into a fight but I must understand at no time and under no circumstances do you ever hit a girl. A good lesson learned at a young age and one that stayed with me up to this very moment. Now at this very moment on this warm June evening I was faced with the possibility of shooting one, one who in all probability is unarmed, one who is probably innocent.)

Although my weapon was trained on the entrance of the center hut I held my fire. I did this for two reasons: the effect from a round fired from an M-79 could only be an indiscriminate one, one that would in all probability have multiple victims; with the earlier presence of women and children I felt it necessary to await orders from the captain. Not surprisingly the orders that came down were for the company to pull back and regroup, take care of the wounded and prepare for a possible assault. Unfortunately for me there was just no way I could move back from my position without being hit. I had no choice. I had to stay put. It became quite clear I would have to make my own decision whether or not to fire into the center hut.

The enemy's arsenal consisted of rocket propelled grenade launchers along with AK-47 assault rifle fire. Since they had a logistical advantage they were successful in keeping a large portion of our company pinned down. This made the pullback all the more hazardous. I wanted desperately to return fire, but I also wanted a clear target. I also knew I had very little time. Cover needed to be provided and needed to be provided now. For a brief moment I closed my eyes and said a quick prayer, "Dear God, don't let me hit any children. Mom, this isn't PS 16." As I opened my eyes and applied pressure to the trigger I was startled by the feeling of a heavy thump on my back. It was Dave Thomas. "You scared the hell out of me," I murmured, somewhat annoyed he had sneaked up from behind, yet at the same time relieved to have his support.

"Your own private war?" Dave asked amusedly as he took aim on the center hut. He then continued, "Did you fire? Do they know you're here?"

"No on both counts," I responded as I swiftly reached out and placed my hand on the barrel of his rifle, pointing it downwards. "Did you know the woman and children are in the center hut?" I whispered.

"Look, everyone knows about the woman and children. What you don't know is that in less than five minutes that center hut is going to be blown from here to oblivion," Dave responded, once again taking aim.

"What the hell are you talking about?" I quizzed.

"The CO just made contact with a passing Cobra gunship on night patrol. He ordered all three huts to be blown. If we can take out the gook with the grenade launcher he may call it off," Dave whispered, then added, "Are you sure they don't know we're here?" I did not respond but instead watched in awe as Dave jumped to his feet, took careful aim in the direction of a rocket propelled grenade launcher that suddenly began to protrude from inside the hut, and opened fire. He then immediately dropped by my side, ejected his empty ammo clip and inserted another as he called out, "Well the fuck'n bastards sure as hell know we're here now." Dave repeated his assault once more, but only after seeing a clear and armed target.

Seconds ticked by with no return fire from the center hut. Then a full minute of silence. Suddenly, the woman carrying the child could be seen making another effort to escape. This time she had not one but two children whose arms were locked tightly around her neck. Although Dave's weapon was trained on the entrance of the center hut he instinctively held his fire. Once again she was pulled back inside. For the time being, the enemy ceased firing. Off in the distance the barely audible sound of the approaching gunship could be heard. "You better tell the CO to call that Cobra off," Dave said to me without taking so much of a glance away from the hut. He was right. I

133

had to get to the captain to apprise him of the situation. For sure I thought he would not allow that gunship to open fire knowing there was a woman and children inside, especially now since the enemy had ceased firing.

With the sound of the approaching gunship getting louder and louder, I knew it was only a matter of a minute or so before it was within strike range. What started out for me as a slow and tedious low-crawl in the direction of the command post now turned into a high speed run. I had to reach the captain before the gunship opened its massive arsenal. As I made my way closer, I could make out the captain who was now within hearing distance, his stare fixed at the now hovering gunship. Looking over at him in the dark of night I screamed out with a might and a passion from within I did not know existed, "The hut, the hut, the center hut has a woman and children." But I was too late. The orders were already given. The gunship opened fire on the first hut, then the middle hut, then the end hut. I watched. I listened. I could do no more. As the captain called a cease-fire he gave instructions and our location to an approaching medevac. We did not get any more return fire from the little village. Later that evening, the 1st platoon did a sweep of the area, cautiously going through the first hut, then the second, then third. With the exception of several dozen rounds of used ammunition along with a left-over enemy rocket propelled grenade, nothing more was found. What became of the women and the children along with the elderly man has, and always will, remain a mystery.

The letter Dave's father received was nothing more than just a letter, one with all the killing and dying and notification that go together with a war which was sent out in error. Dave Thomas was fine. He was also awarded the Silver Star for heroic actions that evening. Soon after he would be offered the distinction and honor of a battle-field commission, one he would turn down. Earlier, it was Dave Thomas who came to my aid and who stayed at my side. I will never know whether or not the effect of his presence kept me from harm that night, or perhaps more importantly prevented me from harming an innocent woman and her children. But one thing I do know. On that evening in June, a bond was created between the two of us and one that would stay with us to this very day. That evening, Dave Thomas was my support. He was my protector. He was my friend.

THE NIGHTS TO REMEMBER

September 1969

Dearest David,

Don't know if you heard but Jimmy Morrone had a car accident after playing golf at the Hudson River Country Club. Injured his knee, hope it won't hurt his game as he is so good.

Got a parking ticket in front of MiMi's in Getty Square…

Love,

The Mother

PS – Walk on the sidewalk

I had been on line for over ten months now. There was a good deal that happened to me in this period of time. There was a lot I had seen and a lot I had done. I witnessed death up close and accepted it as part of the job. I learned to become resistant to or shelve away certain feelings that at one time had been so innate. I discovered I could take the pressures of battle, no matter how intense, no matter what the outcome. I guess the one thing you could say I had not been able to conquer was fear. More specifically, fear of the unknown.

As the captain's RTO, you had to be in the loop, up to speed and always aware of all things happening. The captain gave all the commands and made all the final decisions. For the most part, those decisions were based on information and data supplied to me by the platoon leaders and RTOs of our company and then forwarded on to the captain. If I failed to fully understand or properly interpret the needs and conditions of certain situations or if I misinformed the captain during a run-in with the enemy, the consequences could be unforgiving.

The month of September also brought forth a series of dreams for me. Interestingly, although they were numerous, it was the same dream, just on repeat. One dream I had twice last week and also once the week before. I should talk to Captain Bergson about it, but he may think I am just "shamm'n" (an attempt to avoid going out and into the field).

It was a short dream, perhaps no more than a few minutes. I found myself sitting on top of a bunker inside our base camp with my friend Roger Wasson. Bill Fabricortore, the base camp radio technician sat inside his bunker where he monitored our frequency and that of the battalion's. Miles 'Doc' Touchberry was over in the medical tent making the necessary preparations for what was expected to be a night of heavy casualties.

It was a bit after 8 PM when one of the bunkers located in the northeast corner reported sighting movement approximately several hundred yards beyond the wire. A rocket flare was discharged to light the sky. Although the sighting could not be confirmed, headquarters gave permission to open fire from the bunker. This in turn seemed to have encouraged numerous others to open fire throughout the compound. Shortly after the order for cease-fire was heard, the camp fell into a disconcerted mode. Roger and I did what we could to take our minds off a growing fear that was building from within. A fear and any soldier's worst nightmare was the possibility of an encounter with an enemy force far greater than your own, and being overrun. My dream took me to this place.

As we sat on the bunker Roger would say to me, "All my valuables, including my tape recorder, are locked up inside an empty ammo box located back in Dau Tieng. If anything happens to me would you send it to my home in San Jose?" I assured him I would as he wrote down and handed me his address. Then he would add "How 'bout you? Is there anything that you want me to do for you?"

"Rog, do we really have to be talking about this now because I honestly don't want to be thinking about it?" I would respond. There was a long silence. Perhaps it was due to my nerves being on edge but my attitude and remarks had come across as rather abrasive.

"Look," I added, "I don't really have anything special to be sent home. Just, well, I mean in the unlikely event something should happen to me, just say you were with me and I wasn't alone. I'm not writing this down but I have two sisters, Ann and Laurie, and two brothers, Dennis and Eddie. And of course my mother."

In the dream and over the next few hours it would remain relatively calm. And with the exception of a few officers running around making bunker checks mingled with the constant crackling sounds of heavy radio transmissions it could have been like any other night spent in the confines of our base camp. Except this wasn't any ordinary night. Attesting to that were the rocket flares being sent up every few minutes that lit the sky and campground and surrounding area. There was a sinister glow about them, yet they allowed for good views all the way out to the far-reaching wood line.

"And Jimmy," I said.

"Jimmy?" Roger queried.

"Yeah, Jimmy Morrone," I said.

"What about him?" Roger asked.

"He's my best friend from Yonkers and he should be notified if something were to happen to me," I said.

"All right, so it's your sisters, Ann and Laurie, your brothers, Dennis and Eddie, your mother and your friend Jimmy," Roger repeated.

"And of course Jimmy's sister Kathy along with their mother Mrs. Morrone and her husband, Doctor Morrone," I inserted.

"So it's Jimmy and Kathy and their mother and father you also want notified?" Roger questioned.

"Oh and I can't forget the Leone's, the LePore's and the Strauss's," I added, then continued, "and my friend Steve from New Rochelle and, of course, Al Roberto, he was class President, and also..." Roger now somewhat perturbed quickly interrupted me and yelled out, "Will you shut-up already! I'm not notifying anyone. You're not gonna be killed, McCormick!"

The dream would continue and for several moments we would stare at each other in complete silence. Then almost to the exact second we would both break down in laughter. It was a type of carefree feeling where nothing else mattered to us. We seemed to be transported outside the wire and away from all the surroundings. There was no war. There was no worry. And for a minute or two, our only concern in the entire world was to regain control of our breathing, and for the most part, to enjoy the moment. The time was

137

close to midnight. The dream would continue and in a matter of moments the thirty bunkers that protected the base camp known as Mahone II would come under attack by a battalion of North Vietnamese Army soldiers whose strength would far outweigh ours.

As with any battle, regardless of how well you plan, the very first opening rounds are always a shock. Tonight would be no different. In this dream the fact Roger and I were both lying flat on our backs and recuperating from laughter on top of a bunker probably saved our lives. At exactly midnight the enemy attacked. Bullets, several hundred at a time, raced through the air making a zinging sound as they passed over our prone bodies. All this was accompanied by round after round of incoming mortars impacting throughout the campgrounds. At the same time sections of the campgrounds were peppered with dozens of rounds of enemy rocket-propelled grenade fire. These explosions first landed in the northeast corner of the camp, then the southwest prompting more return fire from our side.

Roger and I would manage to crawl off the top of the bunker located well inside the perimeter and take cover along its side. It was clear the enemy was carefully picking and choosing its target zones in an effort to search out and find the camp's weakest link. It wasn't long before they had found it. One of the southern-most bunkers took a direct hit from a rocket-propelled grenade launcher, killing and wounding several of our men. Despite the numerous layers of barbed wire protecting the outer perimeter of the camp, the enemy, with the help of their own sapper squads, got through. Within minutes a small platoon of NVA soldiers stormed one of our bunkers taking control of it. The time was 12:30 AM. The enemy now was inside the wire.

The struggle to regain control of the lost bunker was fierce. Within a short period of time all the NVA soldiers were killed or wounded. Extra reinforcements of ours were quickly sent in to secure the southern-most area in and around the bunker in an effort to deter any additional assault. From the inner circle of our artillery support group the firing of a steady stream of flares helped us to survey the landscape beyond the wire. In addition several Cobra gunships along with a number of Air Force F-4s assisted in keeping the enemy back. By 1:30 AM, except for a few incoming mortar rounds, the fighting had quieted down.

This attempt by the enemy to overrun the bunker, however, was nothing less than a diversionary tactic. The enemy was nowhere near the point of giving up. They were, in fact, regrouping and readying themselves for one final and massive attack. This time it would be at the northern-most point of the camp. This time they would be attacking bunkers manned by Bravo Company.

As I dreamed on there seemed to be a temporary lull in activity. During this period of time our various defensive positions did everything necessary in anticipation of another attack. With drivers dodging sporadic sniper and mortar fire, Jeeps filled with ammunition and additional weapons made critical drops at each and every bunker.

The dream took me into a new stage of this war, and for the first time ever, I had a serious concern about my own mental well-being. Perhaps this was due to the frequency of them. And if I were to mention it to the captain I would have to talk about the contents of the dream and that would be frighteningly uncomfortable, even after all I had done and after all I had witnessed. I would also have to mention one other thing to him, that the dream's contents were a reality for me and, in fact, had actually occurred on the night of February 22, 1969 almost five months before Bergson had come on line, a night when our base camp had been assaulted by wave after wave of North Vietnamese soldiers.

There was one more reason why I was reluctant to tell Captain Bergson about these nightmares. For the first several months on line the captain maintained a track record that was envied among the various commanders of the 25th Infantry Division. He had enemy kills. He had enemy prisoners. He had uncovered and confiscated enemy weapons and supplies. But perhaps more notably he had yet to lose one man under his command. For a good while the captain enjoyed this winning streak. There was no question, he was riding high. He didn't even have any SIWs (self-inflicted wounds), a compliment to any leader. It would appear, though, part of his reign was a marriage of luck and fate and, as the saying goes, fact is stranger than fiction.

During the early morning hours of September 23, the captain was called off line and ordered to report to division headquarters in Cu Chi for a briefing and discussion on future operations in the area we were currently patrolling, Hua Nghia. A replacement took command of the company for the brief period of time the captain was away. I, myself, took a short leave and had escaped to Dau Tieng. The captain had been gone for no more than twenty-four hours when he was informed one of his men had been mortally wounded out in the field. PFC Shelby Dean Stover, twenty-one years of age, from Ameagle, West Virginia, on line for less than ten weeks, had been reported killed in action. The captain's triumphant streak of good fortune had come to an end.

Later that same evening, in a small dimly lit room attached to the headquarters building, Captain Henry P. Bergson sat down at a rickety old desk. A pen and a blank piece of paper lay in front of him. At the moment he may have been thinking about his men in the field or perhaps even his wife Jackie back in New England. Whatever he may have been reflecting upon, he was alone except for his thoughts. Now Captain Bergson was facing a new challenge. The obligatory letter. A letter sent by all leaders to the next of kin after the loss of a man. A letter that would be written with emotion but also in frustration. PFC Stover was his first loss. Captain Bergson wanted to make sure it would also be his last.

The discussion of my dreams can be put on hold, I later thought after hearing about Stover. I did not feel a need to burden the captain during this time with something I should be able to handle on my own. In addition, I was caught up in my own emotions about this loss, and I found them to be mixed and even at odds with each other. Without question I did feel bad about his death. At least a part of me did. But I also couldn't help but feel I failed myself in not getting to know him or even to get close to him during his brief period on line. My feelings took me back to the very first day in the field when I was introduced to the members of the third platoon.

I thought about the ones who failed to introduce themselves. I thought about others who avoided me altogether. I would soon learn one of the reasons for their anti-social stance was their feeling or belief I would not be around long. Those people were veteran soldiers hardened to the realities and difficulties of dealing with a loss. Past experiences steered them away from making the slightest effort to get to know someone new. The bottom line here is it was easier, and perhaps smarter, to avoid new friendships. Now, reflecting upon the loss of Shelby Dean Stover, I realized I had fallen for and developed that very same attitude. It's not that I avoided being around Stover as much as it was that I had made no special effort in getting to know him, especially since he was new on line. It did not take me long to realize I was no different than those select few men I had seen, but not met, on my very first day in the field. Because of this and for a period of time I took pity on myself. And I was sorry I had not gotten to know him as well as I did many others.

GOING HOME

October 1969

Dearest David,

Called your father to ask him for money to take a cruise. He said no and that I had gotten a good settlement and good alimony. Said to him that if I take a cruise I may meet Mr. Right and get married. Got the check yesterday!
Baves family putting on a show at the Amacassin Club and...

Love,

The Mother

PS – Walk on the sidewalk

There's an expression that time, as we know it, stands still for no one. I'm not about to argue with that. Yet I must say after my first few firefights time, as I knew it, ceased to exist for me. I no longer thought about it. I stopped thinking about days or hours or weeks or months. And as for going home, well that was something that happened to other soldiers. I had been on line for over eleven months. With the exception of a short leave and an R & R, barely a week went by when I wasn't involved in a skirmish, a sniper attack or a heavy battle.

Looking back to that very first day when I arrived in the field and was introduced to John Paxson, Roger Wasson, Pete Arnone and Miles Touchberry, I soon began to realize how very lucky I was. Since the beginning and over time we had all become very close, closer than the typical bonding that develops and takes place in college fraternities, closer than the team camaraderie shared among athletes. We became a sort of rat pack, hanging out whenever possible and exchanging stories about friends and family and, of course, the war. There were times when we discussed our innermost feelings. When we lost someone we acknowledged it. We also respected each other's silence. We knew so many things about each other. We had a sense of comfort and security just by sitting near one another. Now, with only a matter of weeks to go before I would be heading home, I became very much aware I was the only one remaining in the group who had not been wounded or killed.

Captain Bergson had been with us for a little over four months. And I was still carrying the radio. Our missions had changed quite dramatically since the orders from Washington went into effect, changing them from search and destroy to search and clear. It appeared as though we were no longer going on the attack, which was fine with me. Instead it seemed as though we were on the defensive, which added a little extra edge and additional tension among all the troops. From snipers to the Vietcong, from the North Vietnamese Army to the local enemy sympathizers, the enemy seemed to be everywhere. And it was getting more and more difficult to distinguish who was who or what was what.

My second week on line and before I started to carry the captain's radio, a mission we were on had taken me into one of the neighboring villages where we were to take a break. Curious and wanting to learn more about the local people, I took a walk. I soon found myself outside the village perimeter. I was alone and on a secluded path. Suddenly, an elderly farmer rushed up and grabbed me from behind. He was in a state of excitement and shouting in a language that was foreign to me. Tugging at my arm and talking all the while I was pulled deeper and deeper into the brush. We soon came across a clearing. There in the open stood a small makeshift sanctuary that had once contained a statue of a Buddha. The religious figure had been knocked down and was now lying on the ground in front. He was pointing down to it and shouting. Recognizing his dilemma and realizing he was too frail to move it I just leaned down, picked it up and carefully placed it back on the improvised altar. I then removed a bandanna from around my neck and very gently brushed away the dirt encrusted around the statue.

That was nearly twelve months ago. Now, today, I would never dream of doing anything like that. I would now consider a situation such as that highly suspect. The possibility of the old man's being an enemy sympathizer would weigh heavily on my mind. Even the young boys selling watches and trinkets and Coca-Colas were suspicious. But it wasn't just the war that had changed. I had changed. With all the killing and bloodshed and loss of friends and witness to inhumanities I would be ashamed to describe to anyone and can only happen in war, I had changed very much indeed. I was tired. And I knew if I continued to go out on the daily missions, my number would soon be up. I felt today was the day to make my plea to get off line. I felt I had a good case. And I was ready to plead it with everything I had. I also knew I would have a fight on my hands to get myself off line. The captain, I felt, had grown to depend upon my experience and expertise and overall feel for certain situations, especially when things got sticky.

When Captain Bergson first came on line, I perceived there to be a strained relationship between the two of us. I believe the reason for this was due in part to his newness and being a commander. That, combined with my many months of on line experience and having a somewhat "been there, done that" attitude created a little friction between the two of us. It's not that I was cocky. That's not the way I was brought up. But I was outspoken when it came to rules of engagement and the safety of our men. Prior to Bergson's taking command, I witnessed too many situations and observed a number of deaths of our people, from accidents to friendly-fire, that I felt were avoidable or unnecessary. As a result I had become somewhat of a one-man safety advocate for Bravo Company. If I noticed the men grouped together while out on patrols and therefore becoming an easy target I would call a halt and stop the company and have them space themselves out. Often I would do this without asking the captain's permission. Many of the guys had slogans etched on their helmets with indelible ink markers that displayed "The Terminator" or "Killing Machine" whereas I opted to borrow a motto from a highway safety campaign in Florida where I had attended college. Etched all over my helmet were the four letters, B.E.B.A., short for Bring 'em Back Alive.

I believe the turning point in the relationship between Captain Bergson and me came on the front porch of that small colonial manor house during our first firefight back in July. Though only on line for a short period of time, the captain, by asking and taking my advice allowed me to conduct a counter-offensive by the use of an air strike. During this time I believe we reached new grounds of mutual respect. He even laughed at a few of my jokes, and I quickly picked up on his offbeat sense of humor. But there was something else I, along with the other members of Bravo Company, took note of about Bergson. He carried with him an exceptionally high priority when it came to the safety of his men. We had gotten out of the area that day without a single casualty. And from that moment on, we worked together in harmony. Captain Bergson, taking me into his confidence, treated me as an equal and consulted with me on all future missions. I, in turn, learned to admire the man, his knowledge and his wit. It was now up to me to try to break our team. That's why I figured I would have a fight on my hands in asking him to take me off line and allow me safe haven for my remaining time in country.

As I exited my bunker I saw Charlie Company off in the distance approaching the wire. They were returning from an extended ambush mission and I had heard they suffered a number of casualties, including some KIAs. I also noticed the morning convoy had arrived a bit early. It seemed such a bizarre sight to see one of the Division Padre's sitting up front in the lead jeep with a machine gun resting next to him. The trucks came with supplies and with new replacement recruits. This was good for me and my case as I had been informed at least a half dozen of these new recruits were for Bravo Company. For sure one of them had to be capable of carrying a radio, I thought. Crossing my fingers and taking a deep breath I entered the captain's bunker.

Once inside, I was greeted by the first sergeant's blustery voice as he was reprimanding one of our men for falling asleep on guard duty. He was a new recruit. In his defense, I think he was getting the short end of the stick as it was my understanding the recruit had been assigned guard duty several nights in a row and then was put to daytime work filling sandbags and building bunkers. The poor fellow probably had little if any sleep over the past seventy-two hours. Regardless, Top must have felt he needed to put the fear of God in him as he yelled out, "You fall asleep on guard again, boy, and there's gonna be good news and bad news for you. The bad news is that if you're caught sleeping again on guard duty you'll receive a court-martial. The good news is that you'll also face the firing squad and be shot."

Top was famous for this line and I used to think he had it backwards. But if you really knew and understood him, you'd know the way he stated that warning is the way he meant it. Top was a career man. This was his second tour of duty in Vietnam. To him, nothing on this earth could possibly be any worse than a court-martial, even being shot by a firing squad.

I moved past the two of them and pretended to ignore the entire scenario, making a mental note I would have my own talk with this new fellow at some point later on. Falling asleep on guard duty in camp with hundreds of men around you and with at least some activity going on at all hours is one thing. Falling asleep while outside the wire and on ambush where the stakes are higher is another story altogether.

Captain Bergson was seated on his cot studying the S-2 reports that give daily updates and reported sightings on recent enemy activity in the immediate area. He seemed glad to see me and his greeting was cordial as he shared this latest report with me. As I reviewed the information with him I waited for the proper moment to hit him up with my request. Studying the reports he started talking about our next assignment. It appeared the enemy had infiltrated a group of nearby villages, threatening their leaders and attempting to recruit whoever they could to join forces against the U.S. troops. They would make nighttime visits then, with the arrival of daylight, sneak off and hide in the surrounding jungle. Our mission would be to find their hiding places.

At the completion of this impromptu briefing I was caught off guard by the captain's last remark. "I cut your orders requesting an off line position for the time you have remaining in country. If the company clerk doesn't screw up, you should be off within seventy-two hours. Mac, this will be your final mission. You'll be going home soon and we want to get you there in one piece." It took me a moment, but after hearing the phrases "off-line" and "final mission" and "going home," I had to come to terms with the realization these remarks were directed at me. Over the past three hundred and forty some-odd days I had not been one to partake in heavy drinking. Perhaps a few beers here and there. I also was not the type to take drugs nor did I ever indulge in marijuana. That was just not me. Yet now, after hearing what the captain said to me, I was suddenly consumed by a sense of jubilation and ecstasy that could only be greater than all those vices combined. I was also so caught up with emotion I was not even able to get the words, thank you, out to Captain Bergson.

Exiting the command bunker, I thought if there really was such a thing as being on cloud nine, well then I was on it. I was going home! I was going to see my family. My brothers and my sisters. My friends. My mother and my father. I was going home. And except for one more mission, nothing or no one could stop me. I made it, I actually made it. As I walked down the dirt path I had traveled so many times before, I exuded with exhilaration. Heading in no direction in particular and with no destination in mind, I came upon the staging area next to the mess tent where a dozen or so new recruits stood by awaiting indoctrination and assignments. God, they all looked so young. Or was it just the newness combined with innocence.

I stopped for just a moment wanting to give my personal greetings and support to anyone who may have wanted or needed to connect. My mannerism and demeanor, I am sure, could only have come off as that of a five-star general welcoming his troops home after a successful campaign. I spoke to four or five of these new warriors, answering questions as mundane as "how's the food" and "what do you do for showers," "how long have you been on line," "how long before you get off," and "do we sleep on the ground," to questions of a more serious nature such as "how many have you killed," "have you ever been wounded" and "what's it like coming face-to-face with the enemy?"

With my collective experiences I did my best to answer their questions in a positive and upbeat manner. I did not speak of killing. They would find out soon enough about that. Nor did I mention the fact I would soon be going home. After spending some time, our conversations were cut short as a staff sergeant, with a clipboard of assignments in hand, called the group together and began a roll call. As I bid my farewells and exited the area, I made a conscious effort to shake the hand of one of the young fellows who sat in with our little group and yet was the only one that failed to ask any questions. Holding his hand firmly as I shook it, I told him my name and that I was the captain's RTO. I also said to him if he had any questions or if he needed anything, my bunker was directly across from the command bunker for Bravo Company.

I had my reasons for doing this as I had him pegged. I saw the look. I knew the type. It was not just the youthfulness. There was also a purity and naiveté about him. Not the type to think about taking a second look behind some jungle brush that appeared to be moving. Not one to click off the safety on his weapon if only because of an intuitive feeling. Not one to look over his shoulder towards that snapping sound that may, or may not, be coming from an animal. Two weeks, I thought to myself. Possibly three.

But I was not about to let that get the better of me. After all, I could be wrong. Besides, I was still riding high from the captain's news. But this, too, was to be short-lived. Giving a salute in a mocking fashion and bidding good luck to these fresh and inexperienced replacements, I had not been watching where I was going. Accidentally, I backed into one of the men from Charlie Company who had just returned from a mission. I almost knocked him down. I hadn't seen this soldier before. Mud was layered on various parts of his fatigues. His face was unwashed and he had several days' growth of beard. He had a hollowed look in his eyes as he glanced at me briefly. His stare then dropped to the ground. I apologized, as he bent down to pick up something I had knocked from his hand. I stood there and remained very still as I noticed what he had dropped was a dog tag. As he picked it up and brushed it off I could plainly see he was wearing his own set. Again he stared at me. I slowly reached out and gently patted his arm. Once more I apologized, but this time not to him. He continued on his way and left me with the reminder it takes only one mission, only one shot. This was a scene I did not want to be part of. I dropped a notch or two from my station on cloud nine.

Later that afternoon, while lying on my cot inside my bunker, I studied the calendar for the month of November 1969. I thought it was Wednesday, but in fact it was Sunday. So that's why the Padre was visiting this morning, I thought. Counting the days I figured I had exactly twelve left before flying home. I wasn't quite sure how my friend Dave would react once I gave him my news. I imagined he would only be happy for me. We shared this bunker for many months

148

now. During that period of time we grew very fond of each other, sharing stories about our daily missions and some of the many close calls we had together and separately.

Around 4:00 PM I headed over to the mess tent. Not seeing anyone else that I knew I walked over to a table in the far corner where the tent flaps were open and I could get some fresh air. If I had planned it, I could not have chosen a worse spot to sit. Everything happened to me so quickly. Earlier I figured I had been in country three hundred and fifty three days. And it seemed every second of every minute of every hour of every day I had to fight off that feeling of fear. Fear of that final mission, that final shot, that final land mine, that final sniper. It was here and it was now on this 27th day of October 1969 I consciously began to realize I was beginning to surrender to it.

It started with the fellow from Charlie Company I bumped into earlier. He had been walking down the same path as before. It was obvious he had yet to take a shower since he was wearing the same muddy fatigues and had not even taken the time to wash his face. As he passed the mess tent he slowed his pace, then suddenly stopped only a few feet from where I was sitting. He turned in my direction, looked at me briefly then, for the longest time, all he did was stare down at my tray of food which I had yet to touch. It was strange in a way, as he didn't seem to recognize me from before.

Battle fatigue I thought. All the signs and all the symptoms. I had seen someone with this my first few weeks in country but I failed to recognize it as I didn't understand it then. Instead, I am ashamed to admit, back then I just made fun of that person. Thank God this person no longer had a weapon. I was curious why no one had the concern or the foresight to recognize this condition or to be with him. I would think his platoon leader or whoever was close to him should be escorting him to the medical tent. But, then again, maybe it was his platoon leader or friend who was killed, I thought. In any case the hunger pains I was feeling earlier diminished somewhat as I began to lose my appetite. One more mission, I thought. It could just as well be ten times that.

Meanwhile, just a few hundred yards beyond my newfound spectator a LOCH was beginning its descent just beyond the wire. This was a typical and daily occurrence. The passenger was not. On the landing pad awaiting pickup was the scout dog and the handler who had been out with C Company earlier. That did it for me. It was over a week ago, but the sound of the explosion and the words of the RTO from the first platoon still echoed in my ear: "Landmine, we need a dust-off. What should we do with the dog?" It was my good friend Joe Aylmer. He had brushed against the side of a landmine and detonated it. His scout dog Duke was okay. What really spooked me was this was to have been Joe's final mission before returning to Philadelphia. And my final mission would be tomorrow.

I pushed away my tray, got up and headed back to my bunker. En route I succumbed to the imaginations that make up all the fears and nightmares and atrocities that take place in war and I had witnessed over the past many months. My thoughts were all centered on the mission I would be going out on tomorrow. My final mission, after all this time in country, could very well be my final day.

The bunker thickly layered with sandbags and metal and unprotected from the intensity of the sun was unbearably hot inside. The small fan did little to add relief. Not wanting to turn on the single light bulb for fear of adding to the inside heat I just sat on my cot in near total darkness. I felt very much alone and frightened. So many different thoughts played in my mind and this was the one time I thought I had no one to turn to. From a narrow beam of light that trickled through the door I could see the silhouette of my M-16. For a fleeting moment, the thought of what White had done to himself many months earlier crossed my mind. Sitting there in the heat and feeling drained from not having eaten anything all day, I fell into a restless sleep.

Sometime later, a flashlight's beam awakened me. It was Dave. "What time is it?" I asked.

"It's 10:45," he responded.

"A.M. or P.M.?" I inquired.

"P.M.," he said, then added, "Are you okay?"

"I don't know. I think I am, but I'm just not sure," I said to him rubbing my face. I then added, "Did you hear that I am being taken off line?"

"Well, yeah, I heard that this evening at the briefing. I figured that you'd be celebrating or something," he said.

"Well, I think it's a little premature to celebrate," I said as I reached up and pulled the string on our light bulb.

"McCormick, what's with this 'premature to celebrate' bullshit? You're going home." I had known Dave for a good number of months now. During that time we had become very fond of each other. He was my teammate. I never raised my voice in anger to Dave, yet my response to his comment about going home prompted a stern reply. "Yeah, right, in a body bag maybe." Then added, "Bergson has me going out on tomorrow's mission."

"You? Going out on tomorrow's mission?" Dave asked half comically. To which I fired off a sarcastic reply, "Right, Dave, tomorrow's mission, you know — war, gunshots, bullets, bang, bang you're dead."

I guess when you really care for someone you can get away with things like sarcasm and being short-tempered. If I came across as having an attitude with Dave, he took it with a grain of salt and certainly didn't show it. He stared at me for a good moment, then the trademark smirk appeared across his face, almost as if he were holding back a laugh as he said, "Mac, I got news for you. You ain't going out tomorrow. I sat in on the briefing. We're going after three, maybe four platoons of VC. It's an open-ended mission. You're talk'n one week, maybe longer. I heard Sikes has already been appointed to take your place. He's the new command RTO. You're off line fella." It took a few moments to fully absorb what Dave had just said to me. For the longest time there was absolute and total silence in our little bunker as we just stared at each other. Then without the slightest warning I jumped up and darted out the door, almost knocking Dave over as I made a beeline to the captain's bunker.

Pulling open the canvas flaps I entered to find the captain engaged in a briefing and looking over maps with two of the platoon leaders. Top was sitting by the entranceway. The captain, focused on tomorrow's operation, was deep in study and oblivious to my presence. Top just looked at me and held a finger up to his lips, then slowly leaned forward on the chair. With a wink of an eye he whispered in an almost inaudible manner, "You're off line soldier," then gave me a doublewide grin.

"I love you, Top," I whispered back with an even bigger grin.

"Now cut that shit," Top shot back a tad louder than before. Then added, "You're off line but not off my work detail soldier. We'll find something for you to do. How does KP sound?" He gave me a second wink and then a harsh look as he continued, "Or maybe even latrine duty?"

"Anything for you, Top," I said. Then added, "Why, I'd even fix you up with Slash" (a local prostitute who had lost an eye and was once referred to by some of the men as "Cyclops").

The euphoria that was so much a part of me this morning returned. As I walked the short distance back to my bunker I stopped for a moment and looked up at the sky. It was exceptionally clear that evening and I was excited to think these stars shining so brilliantly would be the very same stars I would be looking at in only a few weeks. The only difference is I would be viewing them from the safety and security of my own backyard on Corley Street in Yonkers, New York. As I entered my bunker, I found Dave sitting on his cot looking straight at me holding a bottle of beer in each hand. He knew I knew, and I obviously knew he knew. I was going home. The beer was warm but I managed to down it in only a few gulps.

"You will send me pepperonis," Dave said, then added, "and none of that frozen supermarket shit. You will find a good Italian deli and mail it out to me. Perhaps with some cheese and crackers." With tomorrow's mission only hours away, Dave declined a second beer but offered one to me, stating it looked as though I could use it. I would miss Dave, I thought. He had become a good friend. I would also pray for his safekeeping.

It was close to midnight. The combination of the beers and having not eaten all day had taken its toll as I fell into a relaxed and deep sleep. For the first time in a year, my dreams were peaceful. They were also plentiful as I found myself at the Cape and on the beach at Truro with my sisters, Ann and Laurie, and that sandcastle. I dreamed of my good friend, Steve, from New Rochelle and all the trips we had taken in to New York. I sat next to my brother Dennis and his close friend, John Colt, in our basement family room as they ate pretzels and drank Orange Crush while watching the television shows "Paladin" and "Gunsmoke" on a Saturday night. All, it seemed, was coming my way. I had made it and I was home again.

The first round of enemy mortar fire hit at approximately 3:30 that morning. I was shocked awake from my dreaming and for a moment thought I really was home and in my own bed in Yonkers. From the sound of the explosion I calculated it was within 200 feet of our bunker. The enemy had a habit of pacing their firing at five-second intervals. Experience and discipline dictates under no circumstances do you attempt to run five seconds or more after a round has fallen because there is sure to be another round en route. It may have been the beers along with the fact my focus and attention was to stay alive for only another week or so, but I just kicked open our door and made a run towards the captain's bunker.

I landed with my back up against the inside wall of sandbags next to Top's cot. As strong as our bunker was, the command bunker, I knew, was stronger. A light, partially covered by a handkerchief, cast a dim glow throughout the interior. Both Top and the captain were sitting up on their cots. There were two more explosions but this time farther away and more towards the artillery compound. Seconds later, 105s could be heard returning fire. "Where's your buddy?" Top said as he looked down at me sitting on the floor. In my rush to get to safety, combined with my focus on going home in one piece, I failed to alert Dave. Incoming enemy rounds were a common and sometimes daily occurrence. Ever since we built the bunker Dave and I had weathered some heavy action. One time the bunker had even taken a direct hit. We happened to be out on an operation at the time, yet, upon returning, the only damage done was a knocked over radio along with some sand on our cots. Our bunker had held up well.

By about the fifth round of firing of our 105s, Dave casually walked over and joined us. "What, you don't wake me no more?" Dave's English was fine. That is unless he's annoyed at someone or ticked off at something. Then, it was my experience he would regress to street talk for the purpose of making a point. Combined with expletives, this was a trait that was very much evident in battle with Dave and at times I felt had all the more confused the enemy. ("What, yuz don't show your face?" he'd yell out to the enemy, or "Okay, tough guy, I'll be look'n for you at 3:00 AM on the streets of Danbury.") Dave was obviously a bit perturbed. My response, totally out of character for me, was silence.

153

I failed to wake Dave and I was ashamed to admit it. I was also very disappointed in myself. Because of the small size and layout of our bunker, Dave's and my cots were tandem to each other with mine closest to the door. To have given him a warning, all I would have to have done is stretch over and tap him on the toe, a fraction of a second at best. But I knew what I was doing. I was concentrating on one thing and one thing only. I was counting off the seconds between incoming rounds and worrying about myself only and my run to safety. For a brief period of time we all sat in silence, then, soon after, the firing ceased and we returned to our bunker. Lying there in total darkness I made what must have appeared to be a feeble effort to apologize to Dave. In typical fashion with unruffled feathers he told me to forget about it and it was nothing that warranted an apology. But it did bother me and I couldn't forget about it. Dave was my closest friend. I would, I decided, apologize to him once more in the morning. In addition, I thought, since I was not to be a part of the day's mission, I would get up early and bring him a cup of coffee, something he would appreciate and also, I am sure, would surprise him. At 7:00 AM I was awakened to the sound of helicopters and to the disappointing sight of Dave's empty cot. He had headed off on the mission and I would have to hold my apology until his return.

My first day of battle free responsibilities was a relaxing one and basically I did nothing. I breakfasted, I showered, I walked the compound, I visited a few friends from other companies, and I made some new acquaintances. The greatest challenge was to avoid bumping into Top and the likelihood of a chore or two. But I was successful at that, and as the day moved on I was in search for things to do. By 1:00 PM I decided to strip down to my shorts, climb up onto the top of my bunker and sunbathe for awhile. I realized this might increase the possibility of an encounter with Top. However, the way I saw it was my shorts were an olive green and similar in color to the mound of sandbags that lay about. I figured even if Top, who wore thick glasses, walked by, the probability of his differentiating me from the sandbags was unlikely. Quietly and without detection I lay there enjoying the peace and tranquility.

I found my moods over the next few days to be unpredictable and very often volatile. There were times of the day when I would walk around with an air of arrogance and a sense of self-importance, something that was not part of my makeup and, in fact, uncharacteristic of me. Then there were the days I was comfortable with the reality that I had survived all these months and I was soon going home. I believe these mood swings I was experiencing had not so much to do with the fact I was going home or even the numerous medals I had been awarded but rather with the fact I was, so far, a survivor of this war.

By Wednesday, I seemed to be geared in a state of constant jubilation. The mere thought of going home was almost too much for me to handle. Keeping busy I found was the only way to shield my mind from matter. This was a chore unto itself. At least when on a mission, I thought, the time moved rapidly. But now, it was as if time had slowed down for me. Rarely had an hour gone by when I was not thinking about what to do next. Strangely, and something that made things worse in an odd sense, was the fact the enemy seemed to be maintaining a low profile. We went several days straight without any incoming mortar rounds or sniper fire.

By Friday I hit rock bottom in the boredom department. My interests lay with anything that might give me a little excitement or adventure. It was almost as if I had been going through battle withdrawal symptoms, something that made no sense to me. By mid-afternoon I passed one of the supply sergeants who had just returned from a visit beyond the wire to our local (and only) house of prostitution. Seeing my name on my fatigue shirt he called out to me and asked if I were the same McCormick who was returning stateside. I told him yes. He said I needed to see him at some point for the purpose of returning my weapon, adding, if he were me, he would be celebrating. He then went into detail as to the delights of his across-the-wire visits, something at that time I didn't particularly care to hear.

Later in the day I attempted to catch a little sleep in the privacy of my bunker. Getting rest in the middle of the day I found was a hit-or-miss thing. Sometimes, especially if the various companies were out on missions, it could be deadly quiet. Other times, though, you could be halfway into a sleep and without warning the artillery guns would fire a barrage of rounds in support of one of our units that may have come under attack. In such instances you are shocked awake into a full state of readiness until you have completely acclimated yourself to the surroundings and goings-on. Under these conditions, returning to sleep can be difficult indeed. And although this particular afternoon was a quiet one, the temperature was not cooperating. I was able to get a little rest, yet it was not at all relaxing.

Lying there on my cot, the thought of what the supply sergeant said earlier came back to me. It had been one year since I had been with anyone. Suddenly now, being in a fairly safe and secure position, with my primary thoughts no longer focused on survival, I was allowing myself to think about things like this. The temptation to pay a visit across the wire, along with the desire, seemed to accelerate over the next few hours. What would it be like? I'd heard so many stories. Is this something I needed to do just to satisfy a sexual desire I thought? Or was this just a desire I felt needed to be fulfilled only for the purpose of completing my combat experiences? Getting to the brothel would be fairly easy. I had the rank and the expertise to cross the wire. What appeared to be lacking was the will.

By 6:00 PM I headed over to the mess tent to get a little something to eat. Shortly after I returned to my bunker, grabbed a towel, and headed to the showers to remove the day's sweat and to unwind a bit. The shower area was nothing more than raised floorboards along with a couple of benches where you could place down whatever cleaning articles you might have. Several large water bags, warmed by the sun, were suspended overhead. The area was out in the open and with no curtains. Privacy was a scarcity out here in the jungle, yet the fact that survival and self-preservation was the primary and prevalent focus, the lack of privacy seemed to bother no one. Showering out here in the field was almost as if you were on display in the window of Macy's department store. Looking around at these very odd surroundings I thought in a short period of time all of this would be replaced by the cream colored tiles and shiny chrome faucets that lay within the upstairs bathroom of my home in Yonkers.

Finishing my shower and heading back I observed a senior Vietnamese soldier reprimanding one of his new recruits. They were standing at the small portable water wagon just a short distance from my bunker. The young soldier was what we refer to as a Kit Carson, someone who, months earlier, was considered the enemy and fighting on the other side. He was formerly a Vietcong or a member of the North Vietnamese Army and at some point was either captured or had surrendered. Depending upon the intensity of their beliefs along with the degree of allegiance to their cause, a soldier in captivity may be asked (and often paid) to join our side and fight for us. Needless to say they must first qualify and also attend a series of reorientation programs. Then they must go through a lengthy re-indoctrination. I had no idea what the young fellow was being lectured about but, then again, there were a lot of things I didn't understand about this war. In a short period of time, I figured, none of this would even matter to me.

Once inside my bunker I preoccupied myself with thoughts of what I would pack and what I would leave behind. Basically, there was not much I could take along with me since most everything was government issued. I would leave the fan to Dave. I also had a small portable TV (which received only one station and that was the military channel). In addition I had a small portable radio that was hooked up to a set of helicopter pilot's headphones. Though the sound was not exactly stereophonic, it did a decent job of muffling outside annoyances such as helicopters landing and artillery guns firing.

The approach of evening had done little to cool off the inside of the bunker. Making an all-out effort to cool down a bit I turned the fan on high, switched off the single light bulb and flipped on a flashlight. Minimizing on privacy yet maximizing on circulation, I decided to tie a cord about the door and leave it open. As I sat motionless on my cot all of my efforts to cool down, it seemed, had a negative effect as my body began to work up a sweat. It was time, I thought, to take drastic measures. Dressed in my shorts and grabbing my canteen, I decided to walk over to the water wagon and wet down my head.

Standing alone and to the side of the water wagon was the young Kit Carson soldier. I said hello to him in Vietnamese, which I regretted immediately and realized was a mistake as he responded back with a lengthy sentence I could not even come close to understanding. Ignoring his response I filled my canteen to its top and slowly began to pour water all about my head and shoulders. This in turn triggered a reaction from my observer that made me feel no more than a notch or two above Bozo the clown. Covering his mouth with one hand and pointing at me with the other he did little to control laughter that came across as being nothing less than hysterical. This, of course, prompted me to join in but not before splashing the remnants of my canteen onto him. Holding both hands up in the air and continuing his laughter he shouted out phrases in Vietnamese that again were beyond my comprehension.

One thing about war I thought is it seems to bring out the extreme in people and even sometimes in situations. How so very odd this situation was, I began to think. God willing, in less than two weeks time I will be in New York, with my best friend, Jimmy, downing some beers. And yet, curiously enough, only thirty days ago, there was a good possibility I could have been on the receiving end of a bullet, compliments of my newfound friend. With these thoughts in mind came all the more reason to celebrate. I joined him in laughter and once more filled my canteen and again poured it over my body.

Looking at him again as he indulged in near uncontrollable laughter I couldn't help thinking how the Vietnamese government drafted soldiers that were so young. The same went for the fighting force we had been up against. I had seen captured and dead boys as young as 15, barely freshman-age back in the states. This one couldn't have been more than 16 or 17. He was a nice looking fellow with very soft facial features. The laughter continued for a while then came to an abrupt halt as the sound of a 105-artillery gun suddenly and without warning fired off several rounds. Immediately, the young soldier's body became tense and rigid as he arched up against the side of the water wagon. Dressed with nothing more than a small pair of tattered shorts and with his arms stretched out he was almost reminiscent of a Christ-like figure. I stared at him for a good while not fully understanding the extent of his feelings, then after a moment's time realized he was used to being on the run and on the receiving end of these mighty weapons. "No sweat, no sweat," I called out in an effort to calm him as he stood there trembling.

Returning to my bunker and not ready to go in, I grabbed a towel, dried myself off and then sat outside on top. From there I could admire the stars and enjoy the slight breeze that from time to time would blow in from the distant wood line. Darkness was now all about as the camp settled into its routine evening defensive mode. Sound and movement within the grounds was at a minimum. After a short while it became apparent the young Kit Carson, still standing by the side of the water wagon, was staring in my direction. I wasn't too sure what he wanted as verbal communication of any type seemed beyond our mutual realm. Being new to the camp, perhaps, he wasn't sure where he could sleep. Or, possibly the reprimand he received earlier was reason enough to keep him from returning to his group. Whatever the reasons, I felt sorry for the poor fellow. With that in mind I waved him over to make a last-ditch attempt to see what was going on with him. As he approached, I climbed down from the bunker and reached out my hand to shake his. Pointing to myself several times I said "David," and after a lengthy pause came the reply "Yang," which seemed more Chinese than Vietnamese.

With the fire-mission concluded the camp was once again surrounded by complete silence. The two of us stood there for a moment almost as if inspecting one another. Then, with an inquisitive glance, he peered in through the partially open door of my bunker and spoke something that once again lost me in his native tongue. I think he was not used to seeing a bunker with luxuries such as a fan and a radio, a television and an electric light bulb. Slowly, his curiosity getting the better of me, I showed him in, turned on the light and offered him a seat on my cot. Our communication advanced to hand signals and facial expressions. Clearly there was an excitement about him. He would say something as he pointed out different things that were part of the surroundings. I hadn't a clue whether he was asking a question or making a statement.

The one thing that did seem to captivate his interest was my set of helicopter headphones. Perhaps he believed I might have been a pilot. Noting his interest, I picked up the phones, sat myself down next to him and gently placed them onto his head. His tone and mannerism had calmed considerably since the firing of the 105s a short while ago. He now appeared totally open and trusting towards me. As I reached forward, I flipped the switch on the FM radio and watched in fascination as the rich harmony and pulsating sounds of the song "Monday, Monday," by the MaMa's and PaPa's played in his head. For my little friend this could be nothing less than witnessing your very first snowfall. Watching him escape and enjoying the music, I knew he was not on Cape Cod and on the beach in Truro. But I knew just as well he was no longer in my bunker, or in the campgrounds or anywhere else that might have the slightest thing to do with pain and suffering, with killing and war.

As the evening advanced, we both, it seemed, grew comfortable in the presence of each other's company. He, mesmerized by the music, and I, intrigued by this new adventure. Space was exceptionally tight within the small bunker. Movements for the most part had to be orchestrated. Reaching out and without getting up from the cot we sat on, I took hold of the single piece of rope that secured the door open and gently pulled it shut. The small fan did what it could to comfort our confines. Quietly he sat. Anxiously I watched. For the longest time it seemed the only movement from within was the temperature, as it steadily increased. And even though the solitary electric light did little to add to the heat, I reached up and over his body and pulled the string, which set the tone that allowed us the atmosphere needed for the evening.

THE LAST 48 HOURS

November 1969

Dearest David:

Well your father was married. He had a mission in life but I never knew what it was. Everyone looking forward to seeing you soon. Knew you had what it takes. Knew you could do it!

Was thinking about having...

Love,

The Mother

PS – Walk on the sidewalk

The very first of my exit interviews and debriefings came at 7:45 AM. "You failed to administer a direct answer to a simple question in the appropriate amount of time which creates a motive for me to believe that you are either 'A' not ready to exit this war, 'B' you do not want to leave this war, or 'C' you believe that you are still at war and soldier, this gives me cause for great concern and therefore I am going to restate the question and ask it one more time in a clear and precise manner with the intention of extracting a response and that is when you fired your weapon at the enemy did you ever visualize that in fact you were shooting your mother, your father, your brother, your sister, your captain, your lieutenant, your pet dog." I was lying there on my cot in my bunker, wearing only my shorts and laughing so hard I was sure I would wet myself.

It was only a mock interview jokingly and fondly administered by just a few of my closer buddies, yet I was laughing not so much at the content of what was said as much as the way it·was said. In the military you are trained, become professional and fall prey to the horrors of all horrors, the run-on sentence. I would miss that when I return to civilian life I thought. I was also touched by the fact so many showed up at my bunker to bid their farewells. Members, it seemed from each and every platoon, many, whose names I did not know, came up and stopped by to wish me luck. "Last month you stopped the entire company and called me a goddamn cluster-fuck. You told me to back off and away from the guys around me. You told me I needed to create space and not march so close to everyone because if the guy behind me stepped on a land mine I'd be chopped meat."

These comments came from someone I vaguely remembered, someone whose six foot plus, 200 some odd pound frame now towered over me, someone who looked as if he were about to knock me from here to the landing pad. Looking up and into his eyes and at the same time attempting to conceal my trepidation, I sheepishly asked, "And was that a good thing?"

"Well, someday you'll be a sergeant and I just wanted to thank you now," was his response. Not wanting to prolong this scenario and deciding not to inform him I already was a sergeant, I just told him to take real good care of himself.

Even "Cookie," the short rotund black sergeant in charge of the mess tent, stopped by to bid adieu. "Whenever you were in base camp you always had a kind word to say to me or my cooks about the food we served. You would sometimes say, 'Wow this is like gourmet food.' I knew it wasn't. I knew you were just mess'n with me. But you always said it in such a cheerful and upbeat way. One time you said to me, 'Cookie, I got my M-16 locked and loaded and I'm gonna hold you hostage until you give me this recipe.' That was the day the monsoons ruined our salt supply. You remember that? I knew you were fool'n with me then too. With conditions as they are I know the meals weren't always up to what they could be. But you always had a positive thing to say. And you always had nice things to say. You know I don't even know your name, but one thing I can tell you, you always made my day. You take care now, you paid your dues, you served good, and tomorrow I hear, you're go'n home."

Of all the farewells I received that morning I think it was Cookie's I was moved by the most, probably, because it was so unexpected. In another twenty minutes, the members of Bravo Company would be airlifted out and on to another mission. It was now my time to make the final rounds, to pick and choose whom I wanted to say good-bye to, to bid farewell to those special ones that had become my companions, my partners and my support over the last three hundred and sixty some odd days. Pulling on a pair of pants and lacing up my boots, my first priority was to go in and say good-bye to Captain Bergson, but not before I thanked each of the RTOs I worked with. Ken Sikes had taken over command radio but he was already down the path that led out to the landing zone. I was sorry I was not able to say good-bye to him. Wendell Hannum, a newer RTO from Iowa, gave me a hand shake and a salute. With the tall antennas it was easy to spot all the others. Half dressed and feeling almost out of place, I went down the line meeting up with them and shaking their hands. As the men were lined up and in formation I turned away and in the direction of the command bunker. Well, I thought, let's get this over with. I hated good-byes.

The entrance flap to Captain Bergson's bunker was open and I just walked in. He was alone and gathering together some maps and I guess I caught him off guard. "David!" he said, "Well, I hope you're all packed and ready to go. If the weather is right you could be skiing in New England in another seventy-two hours." I don't really know what I expected from the captain in the way of farewells when I entered his bunker, but it was not a particularly warm one. He appeared somewhat distant to me, almost aloof, and although pleasant as was always the case, he seemed to be talking in clichés and giving pat responses. He was, I realized, also rushed. The sound of the approaching helicopters could be heard off in the distance. "Well, on to another social gathering with Charlie. Sure you don't want to join us for tea? Perhaps some crumpets?" Captain Bergson joked.

Thinking back and considering our closeness I cannot ever recall a time when he openly displayed his true inner emotions. For sure, this would not be one of them. "Choppers spotted," could be heard from someone outside. "Well, David, this is it, I guess. Take care of yourself and drop us a line, you've got our address," the captain said as he hurried out and down towards the landing pad. For a brief moment I had the feeling he was upset or annoyed that I was leaving, perhaps something like a valued player who decides to jump teams prior to a playoff. As he exited the bunker I wanted to call out to him. I was, however, at a loss as to what to say.

163

Off in the distance the twenty or so helicopters could be seen en route to our base camp. The captain, I thought, should have already been out there and waiting. He obviously was running late, a trait that was uncharacteristic of him. About a hundred feet from his bunker and still a good distance from the landing area, Captain Bergson came to an abrupt halt, turned to me, and called back, "Mac." Staring back at him I did not respond but instead waited to hear what he had to say. There was a bit of a pause before he continued, "Thank you." With the intensive cry of "choppers landing" being shouted out, the captain gazed at me, perhaps longer than he had time for. Then just as suddenly as he had stopped, he turned away in the direction of his company and dashed down the dirt path towards the helicopters and the day's mission. It would be the last time I would see him, I thought.

Suddenly, it all made sense to me. Captain Bergson did indeed have feelings. And he did have emotions. He was just shrewd enough and smart enough and strong enough to file them away and keep them under wraps. He was not so foolish a man as to get close enough to anyone who might not be around the next day. The role of commander saddles you with enormous and varied responsibilities. If not fully prepared, the loss of one of your own men can have a devastating effect on you. As a captain you are viewed and judged by your men not only as their leader, but also as their caretaker and protector.

As the helicopters departed, things at the camp quieted down. Top, unlike other command sergeants, had often gone out with us on the missions. On this one he stayed behind to follow up on the monthly reports and, even though I would be out of here in less than forty-eight hours I knew Top was still capable of passing on assignments to me. I quickly returned to my bunker and started to remove some of the photos and small mementos I had collected during the year. With only one exception my thoughts were no longer centered on past events, but instead were more focused on just flying out of here. I knew I was due tomorrow's escape to freedom, had accepted it, and was in fact looking forward to it, with one exception. Even with these past few weeks of being off line, I never had the opportunity to apologize to Dave Thomas for running and not waking him during the enemy mortar attack. This now would have to wait and be done by a letter postmarked from Yonkers.

By late morning I had breakfasted, showered and packed. By early afternoon I learned that a small convoy would be stopping off at our base camp to deliver mail and supplies. Depending on the type of security the trucks were traveling with, and if Top had my papers in order, I considered hopping a ride out of here a day early. My real fear was the possibility of oversleeping tomorrow and missing the morning convoy into town. After careful thought and consideration I felt it would be better to try to avoid Top all together. I decided to make this night my final night at the base camp that had become so much a part of me over these many months in country.

At 5:00 PM I made one final walk around the campgrounds taking in and memorizing as much as I could. Upon reaching the northern-most point where the heavy artillery guns towered over the interior bunkers, I thought back to my very first day in camp at Mahone One when Sergeant Risley cautioned me to not ever walk in front of them. It was good advice. I had in fact experienced first hand what happens to someone when they accidentally walked in front prior to firing when indeed a round misfired. In the past three hundred and sixty four days I experienced so many things. Some good and some bad. Some evil, and many, many heroic. Someday, I thought to myself, I'm gonna write a book about all this.

As I leaned back on the multiple layers of sandbags I noticed two young men walking shirtless out in front. Both were wearing fatigues that were pristine fresh. Their boots were without a speck of dirt, but the real give-a-way was the whiteness of their bodies. Brand new recruits. "Excuse me," I called out to them. They stopped and looked over in my direction. "You really should not be walking in front of the big guns," I said. Both of them slowed their pace a bit and looked in my direction. "Why, they're ours aren't they?" one called back in a sarcastic manner as the other began to laugh. "Well, that's not the point," I said, seemingly talking to the wind as they walked away ignoring me.

Later on I showed up at the mess tent just as they were shutting down for the evening. I went there not so much to eat, but more so to say good-bye to Cookie. The excitement of going home had dulled my appetite. I wasn't really hungry and, of course, Cookie was upset with me. "Take a little something, Sarge, your appetite will come back later, I'm not lying," Cookie pleaded. To which I responded, "You know, Cookie, your meals really were good meals, and I'm not lying."

"God bless you, Sarge, and I'm gonna be thinking about you and I'm say'n a prayer for you that you get home good and safe and with your family where you belong," Cookie replied.

"No, Cookie, God bless you!" I said, then added, "and another thing, you better send me those recipes and I'm serious now." That was my exit line. I had no intention of returning, not even for breakfast.

Heading back to my bunker I was looking forward to spending some time with a few of the guys, one of whom I was led to believe would be there with a six-pack of contraband beers for a final farewell. It was 6:30 PM. The war was over for me. Things were winding down. I had nothing to do but relax and keep myself secure for twelve more hours. If nothing else, the one lesson I learned about war is one that can easily be applied to life — hope for the best and prepare for the worst. Amazingly, as crazy and farfetched as it may sound, in a little over one hour I would find myself outside the confines and security of our base camp and in the middle of hostile enemy territory. I would also be without a weapon. My sole purpose, the rescuing of a friend. And to satisfy a guilty conscience.

A little after seven and as promised, one of my friends, Sergeant Higgins, from battalion, showed up and presented me with a six-pack of beer, two of which were missing. Higgins knew I had taken the loss of medic Miles Touchberry pretty hard back in April, and perhaps for that reason he decided to invite along two of the new medics. Well, I thought, even for a celebration one warm beer is better than none. Higgins slowly and carefully removed each bottle one at a time, calling out, "We have a warm one, and we have a warm one and we have..." and so on. I was introduced to the medics. It was odd in a way, but one of them looked remarkably like Miles. His name was Ron Saunders and he said there was plenty of ice over at the medical tent. "Ron," I said, "you obviously don't know Higgins that well. He's from battalion. They have a king-sized Amana refrigerator. He could have chilled it but he is of English descent, very proper and all and, for whatever crazy reason, the English like it warm."

With the day's shuffling and packing, little as it was, I could not locate a bottle opener. I made a quick dash across the way to see if Top had one. Upon entering the captain's bunker I could see Top was highly engrossed and listening to some radio transmission that was coming across the airwaves. I waited for a break, then asked, "Is that our people?"

"Negative," Top responded, then added "it's a small reconnaissance group, truck, two jeeps, engine problems with the truck I guess. Now they are stuck out there and they've spotted movement in the jungle brush." Since the entire day had gone by without being harassed by Top, I thought it best not to upstage the drama that was unfolding by asking for a bottle opener.

Scurrying back I popped my head into my bunker informing them of my lack of success. Higgins, making a sarcastic comment about my lack of preparedness in a war zone, jumped up and offered to get one from battalion. As he headed out the door I couldn't help but notice an unusual amount of commotion over at battalion. Some were rushing in, some out, others were donning gear and equipment. There were three or four jeeps all armed with M-60 machine guns. For the beginning of the evening and the fact this was inside our base camp the activity was quite unusual. There was no question something big was going down.

Watching all the action I was reminded of the day and time I had resigned as a firefighter with The Seminole Volunteer Fire Department in Florida. The day after, I visited my good friend, Ron and Judy Stiteler at Ron's Auto Sales. They were aware I had just been drafted and Ron was willing to buy back the car he had sold me at a break-even amount. They had become my second family while away at school. As Judy did the paperwork, I noticed off in the distance smoke spiraling up in the area of one of the many large orange fields. Hearing the fire whistle blow and watching as the trucks charged by, I felt a rush of adrenaline throughout my body. Now looking at all the movement over at battalion, I was experiencing that very same feeling. I was no longer a part of this picture and, in a crazy bizarre way, I had mixed feelings about having to leave this all behind. Further, I began to wonder for the first time whether my being here had made any difference at all.

After giving a "Cooke's Tour" and a little history on Dave's and my bunker I took a seat on my cot while awaiting Higgins's return. Within seconds I was hit simultaneously with two very differing questions from my medical visitors. One asked how it felt to be leaving and going home tomorrow. The other asked what's it like during an enemy encounter. "I will answer both of those questions only because you asked," I responded, then continued. "Ordinarily I would be uncomfortable talking to anyone on either subject. I view my feelings about going home this way. It's like I've had some terminal illness and it's been with me and eating away at me for one year and all your focus and concentration and energy is centered on not so much living, but more so on avoiding death on a daily basis. Then suddenly, out of the blue, someone comes up to you, armed with nothing more than a set of papers, and says poof. You're cured. You can go home now. I feel so very fortunate. I know I am one of the lucky ones."

"As for enemy encounters and battles," I continued, "you don't think, you just react. As for being scared, at times, yes. But oddly enough and more often than not you just don't have the time to be scared. You're too busy doing what needs to be done. You do what you're trained to do. And above all you maintain a hope, as little as it can sometimes be, that you will see the sun rise. This war taught me something and that is there will not be one day that goes by me that I will not cherish. Only by witnessing the horrors of war, can you fully appreciate, admire and acknowledge the magnificence and beauty of life."

"Wa-laaaa!" shouted an overly gleeful Higgins ducking his head into our bunker and displaying a real down-to-earth non-military bottle opener. "McCormick," he continued, "when you get back home you send me a case of these openers. We can make a killing." I told him I thought that was a great idea and he should send me a list of items and merchandise that are currently sold on the black market.

"Isn't the black market illegal?" asked one of my new medic friends.

"So we'll call it the Off-Black Market," Higgins chimed in. As we all joked about getting involved in such a venture one of the jeeps that had been over at battalion pulled up out front where I could see two of the guys filling their canteens from the nearby water wagon. The smell of diesel fumes permeated the area.

With bottles opened and toasts completed I stood up, looked out and asked Higgins if he had found out what was going on with all the activity over at battalion. He mentioned they were pulling together a rescue party to retrieve about a dozen or so men from a recon who, as Top informed me earlier, had gotten stuck in a suspected enemy area.

"What type of a reconnaissance?" I inquired, unconsciously feeding my fading rush of adrenaline, to which he responded, "A.F.O." (artillery forward observer). I immediately turned away from the scene outside and gave Higgins a long hard glance.

"A.F.O." inquired one of the medics, "isn't your bunker friend an A.F.O.?" Without taking my first sip, I shoved the bottle into someone's hand and ran full speed across to the captain's bunker. "Top," I shouted, not caring what I may have been interrupting, "the recon mission, the one that's stuck, is that Dave Thomas?" Top, looking up at me with his right ear practically touching the radio's speaker, responded in an annoying steady monotone, "It would appear so." He then turned away and focused on the continuing transmissions.

The decision took less than a mili-second. My best friend was in trouble. The beginning of a rescue mission was in progress. I would be a part of it. The atmosphere reeked with a sense of urgency as orders and directives were shouted out among the rescue party. Listening to all this it seemed as if I was back in Seminole, Florida after hearing the fire whistle go off. Only this time the truck would stop for me. I made a mad dash from the command center back to my area. As I approached my bunker something suddenly dawned on me. Twenty-four hours earlier I had relinquished my weapon. I stopped and froze in place just inches from my bunker. Going outside the wire, after nightfall, into an area of suspected enemy movement and without a weapon had more than a slight trouble indicator attached to it.

Shelving these thoughts and pulling myself together I casually rejoined my three-some and stood there for just a moment. My personal thoughts were reduced to a seesaw-like mentality that was working overtime. *Dave, you owe this to him. Dave, tomorrow you are going home*. With the orders "Let's go people" being called by someone just outside my bunker, my mind was made up. Reaching over Higgins and grabbing my helmet and without looking anyone in the face I calmly asked, "By any chance… does anyone of you…possibly have… an extra weapon, that I could borrow?" Getting a silent response I turned to them only to observe a look of total bafflement on all three faces. "No, I suppose not," I said, then continued, "well then, wish me luck."

In an instant I was out of my bunker and sitting on the back end of a jeep next to an M-60 machine gun operator. Up front were a driver and a lieutenant. We were at the tail end of a five-vehicle convoy consisting of four heavily armed jeeps. There was also one small truck, empty except for the driver. Our engine was revving up and we were ready to roll. I did one final glance around me and spotted my three companions standing outside of my bunker. They were still speechless and appeared to be in awe of the goings-on. "Let's roll," came the order from the lieutenant up front. The lead jeeps, along with the truck, had moved up earlier and were now waiting for us at the gate. Suddenly, as we jerked forward, a voice, seemingly from nowhere, bellowed out, "Halt!" It was Top.

Except for extreme and extenuating circumstances it would be highly unusual for someone of Top's stature to call an order, any order, without first getting the approval from the officer in charge. There was no doubt Top was the highest ranking, but it was a ranking of non-commission. The lieutenant on the other hand was the lowest ranking. Then again he was commissioned. He was the officer. Therefore, it was the lieutenant who was in charge and had the final say on everything. Yet as is often the case and in most instances a healthy respect and mutual understanding existed between most officers and the first sergeants. You don't become a first sergeant without hardened on and off line experience. However, if the young lieutenant were to have given Top the slightest indication of displeasure over orders called without his permission, Top, being the career soldier he was, would have acquiesced. With the jeep skidding to a stop, the lieutenant said nothing.

"And just where on this man's earth do you think you're going soldier?" Top shouted out while staring directly at me. I was caught and I knew it. Not running into Top all day long was just too good to be true. Had I been prepared or had a little more time I would have had a good cover story for him and in all likelihood would have, with a little finesse, bull-shitted my way out. But at this point, there just wasn't any time. As I sat there looking at Top, a small crowd started to gather around, few of whom I knew. I figured most hadn't the slightest idea what was going on. There appeared, however, to be a tremendous sense of curiosity about what was taking place and I suppose the reason for this was quite simple. The fact is the overwhelming majority of the people in the camp were quite content and would do whatever it takes to stay within the wire. Now, here was this one crazy fellow finagling to go out. I knew I was being challenged. I also knew I had to meet my challenger head-on, yet with the crowd growing, do it in a respectful way.

"Top, I'm going out for Thomas," I pleaded in a very authoritative way.

"Not over this top sergeant's dead body," Top retorted. Top's tone and demeanor were like nothing I had witnessed before. But more than that I detected a sense of finality in his voice. He did not want me to go out. I, however, was determined to be a part of this rescue mission. With his mood and his mind-set, along with the tensely rising atmosphere, I knew I had only one shot at a comeback. Picking and choosing my words very carefully and coming across with a somber undertone I called back, "Top, do you think that there is any way that you can stop me? This is my best friend. We fought side by side. You of all people know that. He's out there now. And he's in trouble." There was no response from Top so I continued. "Just answer me this. If the tables were turned and it was your friend out there, what would you do?"

The crowd seemed to be frozen in place awaiting a win or lose response from one of us. "Sergeant," the lieutenant called to me as Top turned away and retreated into the command bunker. "Your first sergeant seems to have made himself quite clear, I need for you to dismount. Your friend Thomas will be okay." Not winning Top's support was one thing. Not gaining the lieutenant's permission to go was quite another. My options were now non-existent.

As the crowd began to disassemble I felt a need to give it one more shot. "But lieutenant," I said.

The lieutenant unceremoniously cutting me off shot back, "I'm sorry sergeant, I don't have the time to argue. Top gave a clear and decisive answer and I..." As the lieutenant's voice trailed off to a whisper, the intent look he had portrayed slowly melted away to a smile. Following the lieutenant's gaze and turning behind me I locked eyes with the first sergeant. In his hands was a military issue bulletproof flack jacket. Without the slightest bit of dignity Top took the jacket and shoved it into my lap. "Don't you have me write a goddamn letter!" Top said to me in a barely audible manner.

"Okay, driver, let's move it, we've got people out there," shouted the lieutenant. With the engine revved up and the jeep moving forward Top called out, "I would have gone." Not quite sure what he meant I shouted back, "What's that Top?"

"If he were my friend, I would have gone," Top yelled. Within moments we were at the wire, an instant later we were beyond it. We moved along the uneven dirt highway at top speed, our headlights in the off position. The warmth of the evening air blowing about my body was rejuvenating. It also helped me to take my mind off what I had just done, especially the part about Top's not wanting to write a letter trying to explain to my family how, only hours prior to boarding a flight home, I was killed.

There was a lot of chatter among the passengers, especially the machine gun operator. It was the type I referred to as nervous chatter, those unneeded but often necessary conversations that take place before going into battle, the sole purpose of which is to let someone know you are, for the moment, alive and well.

"May I ask you a question sergeant? What was that all about?" yelled out the machine gunner who was standing upright and holding on for dear life.

"It's a long story, but a friend of mine is out there and I want to be one of the ones bringing him back."

"May I ask you another question? Where is your weapon?" the gunner queried. I shouted out, "I had to relinquish it." The lieutenant was quick to chime in, "No weapon? Oh wonderful. Okay sergeant what's your story, what do I have, an SIW or an AWOL?" (absent without leave).

"You have someone going home lieutenant," I responded.

"Sergeant, when I worked in S-4 (supply) you were allowed to keep your weapon up until the day before you left country," the

172

lieutenant shouted, then turned to me and added, "since when did they change that policy?"

"They didn't, sir, I'm going home tomorrow," I responded. The lieutenant quickly turned away from me, did a brief acknowledgement of expressions with the driver, and then stared forward in silence. The gunner, suddenly mute and at the same time avoiding eye contact with me, took a rag and began wiping the dust that was now gathering on his weapon.

I couldn't really tell how fast we were going but it was a good clip. It was also pitch dark and everyone knew this was "Charlie's" time where the camouflage of night allowed him to plant and cultivate his harvest of road mines. I hoped it was a bit too early for the enemy to be conducting this type of business. We were told the stranded vehicle and its crew were less than ten miles from our base camp. It seemed for sure we had traveled that and then some already. There was a noticeable tension among all of us, and it was not just the concern about a nighttime enemy encounter. I am sure if the lieutenant had known at the outset I did not have a weapon, he would have prevented me from going. Armed, I was an asset. Now I was a potential liability. What was I thinking to have volunteered, I wondered? Where was my head? Did I honestly think, by surviving all these days on line without taking a bullet, I could escape being harmed and safely complete one more mission? I would need more than both hands to count the number of guys I knew personally who got hit just before going home.

With the jeep in front beginning to slow, the lieutenant grabbed the radio handset and held it to his ear. "Okay, the recon is sighted up forward," the lieutenant called out, then continued. "Gentlemen, here is the game plan. We have a mechanic in the lead jeep, he will have five minutes to assess the situation and conduct the necessary repairs, if he feels it will take longer we abandon the vehicle and return to the base camp." Our vehicle slowed to a crawl. The lieutenant went on, "Sergeant, what's your name?" A morbid thought flashed through my mind. It's on my dog tags. "McCormick, sir," I said, to which the lieutenant responded, "Sergeant McCormick, this is a rescue mission. The vehicle you are riding in is a military issue M-51 jeep. It is not your white horse. Do I make myself clear? You will stay with the vehicle. If we hit any shit, you feed ammo to the gunner.

Understood?" Being out here in the dark of night, in unfriendly territory without a weapon to defend myself is analogous to being in New York City's Herald Square in the middle of rush hour without a stitch of clothing, I thought, but more serious. "Yes sir," I responded.

The light of the moon now allowed us some good visibility. As we came to a stop, the broken-down vehicle could be seen off to the side of the road, stranded and with hood open. It was a much larger truck than the one we had brought along, yet there were only about fifteen to twenty men milling about. The lieutenant along with the driver dismounted and met up with the officer in charge of the recon mission. Not seeing Dave I wanted to get out and look, but I sensed the lieutenant's earlier order was one order that should be followed. I stayed with the vehicle and kept a sharp eye out and about the wood line. I was also checking my watch. Five minutes was coming up when the lieutenant approached our vehicle. "Find your friend Thomas?" he asked.

"Negative sir," I responded.

"What's his first name?" the lieutenant inquired.

"David," I answered. The officer then turned and called out, "Is there a David Thomas in the group?" In the shadows of dusk and only a few vehicles forward a voice called out, "I'm Thomas."

"Well, front and center, Thomas," the lieutenant barked, then went on, "It appears that you have someone here that thinks enough of you to pull together an entire mission for the sole purpose of rescuing you. Soldier, you must be pretty special and I would say that a thank you would not at all be out of line."

To say the least, the lieutenant's humor was kind indeed and, had it not been for the time of day, you would have easily seen the blush forming upon my face. From the distance and where he stood Dave hadn't the slightest idea who was sitting in the back of the jeep. As he moved forward the shadows concealing our identities slowly melted away. And as recognition set in, Dave's trademark smile cast a glow that acknowledged all was well between us.

"And you're leaving tomorrow," Dave said with comic sarcasm, then continued, "So what's a guy like you doing in a place like this?"

"I just needed to find out if the pepperoni I'll be sending you from the states should be plain or spicy," I responded. From a distance down the road I could hear orders being called, "Mount up, mount up,

174

mount up. The truck stays behind for Charlie. We're out of here." Within moments our driver along with the lieutenant were back on board. Sitting next to me as we moved back up the highway at top speed was my friend, Dave Thomas.

We returned safely to the base camp that evening. I never did follow up with a second apology to Dave. With everything we had been through all these months and right up to this evening's incident I felt it wasn't necessary. Equally we had stuck our necks out for each other and watched each other's backs. But we were friends and that is what friends are supposed to do. That night, my last night went by like a flash, and at 5:45 AM, Top was tapping me on the shoulder informing me the convoy for my trip back was running early and I should get a move on. Dave's bunk was empty and I was not sure where he had gone.

By 9:00 AM I was en route to headquarters for my final and for real in country debriefing. Surprisingly, everything that day moved very quickly and almost like clockwork. Although I was able to take a shower before boarding the plane, I was not given a clean pair of jungle fatigues. The ones I had on were considerably faded from the strength of the sun and the time spent on line. They also had some dirt and a lot of dust on them from last night's outing. The plane I boarded was similar in size to the one that had brought me over. The passengers, the majority of whom were wearing their fatigues, were quite different. Unlike the initial trip over, this one was considerably more quiet. What little conversation there was appeared to be upstaged by quick glances that were often mixed with long stares. I sensed there was extra baggage on board, and not all of it was neatly stored away in the compartments below. There was little doubt an awful lot was on everyone's mind. I slept as much as I could and, after making one refueling stop in Anchorage, we landed in Oakland, California. We were ushered off and sent to a holding area for the purpose of medical checkups and one more debriefing.

The holding area was actually a large indoor basketball court. Each side had ten sets of bleachers that could accommodate approximately thirty people each for a total of 300 on both sides. As we entered the large arena I noticed the bleachers on one side were already filled, perhaps from an earlier flight. All were wearing jungle fatigues. We were greeted by several officers and ushered into the empty bleachers opposite the ones across the court. After everyone on our side was seated, one of the officers stepped forward and asked for our undivided attention. He then began to read off a list of various items that were considered contraband and cautioned us if anyone were to be in possession of these articles they would face stiff penalties including fines and possible imprisonment if caught. The list was quite long and covered items from drugs to weapons.

I really paid little attention to the officer, as doing anything illegal was just not my thing and, therefore, this did not pertain to me. What I did appreciate and take notice of was we were in a building that was located in California and very much on U.S. soil. I was not in Yonkers, or Westchester or New York, yet I felt I was home. There was something else that caught my attention, and it was directly across from me. It hadn't really dawned upon me at first, all the looks and stares our side was getting from the soldiers on the opposite side of the court. Then I noticed. Their fatigues gave them away. And their boots. They were brand new. These were not combat veterans but rather our replacements awaiting their flight to South East Asia.

After a moment's time it was obvious I was not the only one in our group that had noticed this fact. Comments, many of which were sarcastic and off-color, could be heard from some of the battle seasoned veterans. One of the senior officers, quick to pick up on this, interrupted the one reading from the list and warned us in a hushed manner he would personally court-martial anyone he caught making the slightest derogatory remark to the soldiers sitting across from us. As the reading of the list continued, so did the stares, from both sides. Soon after several sergeants came out and stood directly in front of the new replacement recruits. One of the sergeants, in unison with one of our officers, called out orders for everyone to fall into formation. Our group was facing the direction where a team of medical personnel sat behind some curtains. The group of new recruits was facing the doorway we had originally entered where the trucks that were parked would be taking them all to the nearby airfield. As the last set of the bleachers consisting of approximately thirty new recruits emptied, I could not help but think: that's how many it would be that would not be returning from that group.

Movement on line was slow as I awaited my medical checkup. I scouted up and down looking for someone, anyone I could relate to.

After about an hour of being in line, a corporal standing in front turned to me and said in a pleasant Southern drawl, "You know, it's strange in a way."

"What's that?" I asked.

"Well," he continued, "we've been here in the U.S. for what, four hours or more. I've seen officers and military personnel and even a few civilians come and go. I mean, don't get me wrong, some were real nice and all, I just find it a bit odd that's all."

"What are you talking about, what's so strange and what's odd?" I inquired. The Southerner then turned to me and stared directly into my eyes and said, "Well, no one has said welcome home. I mean, it's almost as if they are ignoring the fact that we were over there. I'd like to hear someone, anyone, even a civilian just say to me, hey, welcome home. That would be nice."

"They will," I said. "They will. Just give it time."

David William McCormick

RTOs Ken Sikes (L) and Alan Hicks

Smoke marks the spot for airlifted out and return to base camp. Note the Cobra gunship patrolling the area.

Grounded Cobra gunship after the "friendly-fire" incident.

David William McCormick

Rare moments: Bathing under watchful eye.

Me on the right and Dave Thomas.

The "High-Five" with just five more weeks in country.

Village children with their "General"

Miles "Doc" Touchberry, Jr.

Donovan (R) on lookout only days before being hit.

Captain Fred Wong, (L) maps in pocket, cigarette in hand, thumb up, taking a call, ready to roll.

Captain Wong in the command center.

Captain Wong, now a General (Ret) and me, 33 years later.

Captain Wong 2nd day of the riverboat operation and only hours before I was ambushed.

Captain Wong ponders as he prepares to sample one of John Paxson's culinary experiments.

Captain Henry P. Bergson

RTO Alan Hicks

The house where Captain Bergson and I were attacked.

Joe Aylmer of Philadelphia and his scout dog Duke.

John Paxson walking by Division Headquarters. The boat in front is one that was discovered by our company.

My friend Roger Wasson, taken a few weeks before he was wounded and sent to Japan.

The beauty of a Saigon River sunset.

What a land mine can do to a tank.

33 years later (left to right) Captain (General Ret.) Fred Wong, me, along with RTOs Alan Hicks, Ken Sikes and Wendell Hannum

Visiting the Wall (left to right) - Ron (Gramps) Risley, Danny (The Tunnel Rat) Hughes, Peter Arnone, Ron (Fuzz) Olsen, me, Charles (Hatch) Hintzen, Fred Wong (kneeling)

Our wreath to honor those who did not return.

Door gunner

Dave Thomas inspecting aftermath of a road mine.

David William McCormick

Riverboat patrol

Eagle flight

Being entertained by Bob Hope.

Farmer tending a rice paddy during monsoon season.

Dave Thomas taking a break outside of the Command Center.

Building one of our Fire Support Base camps.

Mama-san balancing food and child.

Monsoon season

Left to Right; Me, Dave Thomas, Ken Sikes, Wendall Hannum

Captain Henry P. Bergson

A mortar attack at the entrance of Saigon.

Enemy POW taken in for interrogation.

Wood line of the infamous Michelin Rubber Plantation.

More than just the enemy to worry about.

**Medevac; average amount of time between being hit and being transported to a
medical station was less than 30 minutes.**

Collecting enemy munitions one day after the February 1969 massive assault on our base camp at Mahone. Captain Wong and John Paxson.

Me (L) and John Paxson during 24 hour "time out."

Pete Arnone (R) taken shortly before he opened fire on 4 enemy point men. He would survive, when only moments later, a rocket propelled grenade would saturate his body with 32 pieces of metal.

Pete Arnone with his M-60 machine gun.

After hours of taunting our entire company an enemy sniper is taken out.

Printed in the United States
1071200003B/301-306

9 781403 365538